Mastering the Art of
DICTATION

Mastering the Art of

Gulf Publishing Company
Book Division
Houston, London, Paris, Tokyo

DICTATION

Auren Uris

Mastering the Art of
DICTATION

Library of Congress Cataloging in Publication Data

Uris, Auren.
    Mastering the art of dictation.

    Includes index.
    1. Dictation (Office practice) I. Title.
HF5547.5.U74   653'.14   79-27892
ISBN 0-87201-171-2

Books by Auren Uris

Techniques of Leadership
Action Guide for Job Seekers
The Executive Deskbook
The Executive Interviewers Deskbook
Executive Dissent-How to Say No and Win
Over 50
Mastering the Art of Dictation

Acknowledgments

Many people have contributed to my understanding and appreciation of the art of dictation. When I became a staff member of the Research Institute of America, I worked with the department's editorial assistant, Elise Golden Kellison, now of La Canada, California. Elise was both patient and encouraging, and with her help my dictation skill rapidly blossomed. A succession of secretaries helped further to sharpen my abilities in that same area.

I want especially to express my gratitude to the late Herb Popper, editor-in-chief of *Chemical Engineering,* for accepting my suggestion that I write a how-to-do piece for his publication. That article was the seed from which this book derives.

Colleagues at the Research Institute offered constructive criticism that helped the planning and completion of the work, especially Jane Bensahel, Ruth Burger, Pat Durston, Tom Quick and Barbara Whitmore.

I am much indebted to Madeline Cohen, C.B. Hayden, and Nancy Rock, of the Research Institute library for their most expert professional guidance.

For help with the preparation of the manuscript, my thanks to Charlotte Braunhut, Doris Horvath, Judith Goodman, Ann LoMele, and Morna Douglas.

And of course, special recognition is due the people who collaborated in the dictation workshops that were instrumental in pretesting the principles and techniques of dictation described in these pages, especially William Hasslinger, Mary Ann Jung, Marjorie Noppel, Joe Neuwirth, and Bob Winterhalder.

And finally, I thank Doris Reichbart, whose continuing interest and reassurance made the planning and writing of this book a less solitary, and even a happy undertaking.

Contents

Part IV. Increased Excellence

11. Sharpening Your Skills, 121

12. Additional Uses of Dictation, 135

Important Features in this Book, 142

Index, 143

Preface

I am the author of over 30 books. All but the first two have been dictated. After the long ordeal of producing the first and second by a combination of longhand and hunt-and-peck on a typewriter, I decided there must be a better way. I tried dictation, and after a shaky start, began to develop a skill which, after some years, became the mainstay of my professional writing. Further, I developed a systematic approach to *talking* the written word, and it is essentially this system that is described in the chapters ahead.

The timesaving amazes people. Friends, colleagues, acquaintances ask, "Where do you find the time to do so much?" Their perplexity arises because, in addition to my freelance book writing, I am a full-time staff member of the Research Institute of America, a business publishing and advisory service. Depending on the circumstances, I will answer: "Magic wand" or "I use a computer" or the real explanation, "I dictate."

I had wanted to do a book on dictation for some time. My eyes had been opened to its tremendous promise after I did an article for *Chemical Engineering* titled "How To Dictate," reflecting my successful use of this technique. There was a happy surprise in store for Editor-in-Chief Herb Popper and me. After the article appeared, the magazine received more requests for reprints than they'd ever had for a management piece.

In addition, several other business journals including two from abroad—Italy and France—also ran the article. These magazines also were flooded with requests for reprints.

Pleased, but puzzled by the popularity of the piece, I finally came up with the logical explanation: ''Of course. It's the *immediate* increase in effectiveness. Take a skill like decision-making, or how to motivate people, both important in business. There are wide audiences for these subjects, which are read with the hope that *eventually* there will be some gain. But with dictation, as soon as you establish your ability, *there are immediate payoffs*—among others the saving of time.''

The Dictation Workshop

In preparation for the writing of this book, I conducted a training workshop to teach the methods I had developed over the years. I felt that this experience would not only test my techniques but would also help to develop new insights and information regarding the dictation process.

The workshop approach improved the dictating skills of the participants—a group of professional business people who used dictation or did writing—in their jobs—and also brought the advantages I was seeking. Accordingly, the chapters ahead reflect material that has been pretested, and include information and insights that result from adapting my methods to the needs of others.

This book puts into the hands of people who communicate by the written word—executives, managers, engineers, technicians—yes, and you can add professional writers—pretested techniques by which they can make dictation a dependable skill. And once mastered, this capability brings tangible benefits.

Some Words About Words

People who dictate are a unique group, and as language has a way of doing, special words have appeared by which the group is designated.

One usage, which I avoid, is to call the person who "writes out loud" a *dictator*. Like many, I find the word has a pejorative sense that makes its use undesirable. I much prefer the word *dictater* (a common way of creating nouns from verbs is by adding *e r*). Accordingly, you will find *dictater* the designation most commonly used in this book.

With the rise of word processing, two other designations have become common:

Word originator. This phrase, somewhat cumbersome, does have a logic in the word-processing context. While a secretary is not likely to refer to a boss as a "word originator," it isn't too far fetched for a person in the word-processing unit to think of the person behind the words on a tape or other medium as a "word originator." You will find this phrase used from time to time in this text.

Author. Also derived from the word-processing milieu, this designation is an attempt to use a more graceful word than word originator, or another usage, "originator." While *author* suits the world of business, it has the virtue of brevity and an aura of the creative effort. Accordingly, this term also appears in the pages that follow.

And finally, in Chapter 2, the word "dictationese" appears. The reason for this coinage is to make clear that the language that dictaters, word originators, and authors speak is *not* the usual form used in other types of communication. *Dictationese* is the name for that peculiar, but purposeful tongue that those who "write out loud" learn in order to achieve effectiveness. Once the rudiments are understood, dictaters find that it becomes a comfortable second language that helps greatly in getting exactly what is wanted down on paper.

Auren Uris
January, 1980

Dedication

*To the cause of better written communication,
to which mastery of dictationese by the population
at large can make an important contribution.*

Part I.
Dictation and You

1.
What You Stand to Gain

We are all potential dictaters. Anyone who can speak can dictate. And with the proliferation of word processing, more and more people have the opportunity to "write" by dictating either to a secretary or a recording machine.

A Skilled Dictater in Action

Manager Peter Bramble, holding a written query just received from the front office, dials the three-digit access number that puts the recorders in the word-processing department at his command. Briskly, he provides the information the transcriber will need to type the material in the proper format. Then Bramble begins the body of the memo: "To C.R. Castor (he spells out the name). In reply to your question about the drums piled up in the hallway of Building B, (as in boy, comma) I'm happy to report that they've just been removed, period. Signed Pete Bramble."

He doesn't have to bother spelling his name or adding the date or department location. Both typists in word processing are old-timers and will take care of those details. Then he goes on to dictate a few short letters.

Bramble is an effective dictater, spends about a half hour a day at it—sometimes more, sometimes less. In this brief time he is able to turn out a large volume of memos, outside correspondence, and an occasional lengthy report.

Peter Bramble says, "Until I learned to dictate, this same material took much more of my time. I don't think it is a coincidence that I have been given more high-level responsibility in my job."

The time-saving of dictation is evident when you consider some figures: the person who sets out to do a report in longhand can probably produce it at the average rate of 30 words a minute. Dictated to a capable stenographer, that speed would triple. And if a machine were used, dictaters could get down their thoughts almost as quickly as they could find the words for them.

> Peter Bramble, our typical dictater, says, "I have reduced my preparation to a minimum. As a result, my communication has a free-swinging and informal quality that makes it more effective."
>
> "One afternoon," he continues, "I was planning to leave the office early to fly to our other plant in Chicago. My boss came in : 'Can you do a report on the status of the new customer service contract? Mr. James is meeting with members of the board tomorrow morning and he's anxious to get the information.'"
>
> Bramble went on, "In half an hour I was able to dictate all the information the president needed. I would have had to change my plans if I had not been able to put the information on tape quickly."
>
> With all loose ends of his week's work tied up, Bramble boarded a plane to Chicago. Thinking of the week ahead, there were a number of ideas he wanted to remember and actions he wanted to start when he returned to the office. In the relaxed atmosphere of the Chicago-bound plane, Bramble used a pocketsize machine to record all the ideas and messages he had in mind. When he got back to the office on Monday, he simply sent the tape to word processing.

Some people are able to dictate better than others. But, it doesn't necessarily follow that the fluent speaker is the one who makes the better dictater. In some cases, the less fluent may actually be dictating "harder" copy: If thinking is orderly, dictation may be more concise than that of the people who speak easily, but whose thoughts meander.

Potential Gains

The ability to dictate is becoming essential in today's business environment. The advantages assume major proportions as skill increases. Those who achieve mastery can be assured of the following benefits:

1. Time-Saving

The percentage of time saved by dictating rather than writing the same material in longhand or even by some degree of proficiency with a typewriter can range from a minimum of 25 percent to 85 or 90 percent. The reasons for this jump in efficiency of communication is that people generally can speak more quickly than they can write. A contributing factor to time-saving, however, has to do with the mental mechanism by which people put thoughts into words.

2. Flow of Ideas

People who master the ability to dictate will find they "write" more fluently, more freely, and more effectively, and express their thoughts more cogently than those who seek to put the same ideas down on paper directly. And for some people who "can't write" (this includes a surprisingly large number of professionals both at the management and technical levels in organization life), dictation can help break a writer's block. For example:

An engineer was asked by a business journal to write an article about an improvement he had been able to make in a manufacturing process. Weeks passed, and though he and the editor of the journal had gone over the subject and had even developed an outline, the engineer couldn't set pen to paper.

Finally, in my role of both friend and professional writer, he came to me for assistance. I suggested, "Why not dictate your piece into a dictating machine? Using this method you won't be 'writing'—the thought of which seems to stop you. You'll be talking—something you've been doing all your life." And I added a few practical tips.

My friend went off with a tape recorder and his outline. He came back the next day, beaming. "I dictated the whole article in an hour's time," he said. "It's now being transcribed."

3. Career Help

A special point about this engineer's feat: Dictation can give you a career booster shot. Whether you're the treasurer of your company or a department head, if you can write about what you do, you can increase your status and reputation. For almost every discipline and technical area there are professional newspapers, magazines, and journals. If you have something to say, some special interest or achievement, or want to discuss the ethics, philosophy, or some practical aspect of your chosen field, you can make your mark among your peers by writing—that is, dictating—what you have to say. In short, if you want to make it in print, the ability to dictate can be a major assist.

In a somewhat smaller but no less important arena, you can win both ego-satisfying and career-building status by submitting articles to your house organ or publications of your local professional chapter.

4. Fit in Rush Writing Jobs

Remember how Peter Bramble was able to quickly deliver the information the company president wanted? This capability, while not frequently needed, comes in handy in special situations. And your ability to deliver on short notice is generally looked on as a sign of flexibility and competence.

5. Use "Deadspots"

People who dictate, and couple this skill with a small pocket recorder, can use time that ordinarily is non-productive. No one will argue the virtues of just relaxing or thinking, but when you're stuck in a station or airport, you're traveling and the pleasant sensations of movement begin to pall, then dictation ability plus the pocket recorder can put you ahead of the game. They help you record ideas that might otherwise disappear. Of course, it's possible to write in longhand under some of these conditions, but the physical situation—a bumpy road bed or a minimum of elbow room—may cramp your style; not the case with dictation.

One executive's dictation practices are revealed in a biographical sketch:

> A little white car motors north along greater Boston's interstate beltway, Route 128. It's 7:30 a.m., but the driver is oblivious of the trucks and cars sailing past. Although there is a CB antenna on the trunk, the small black box in the driver's hand is not a CB microphone. It is a pocket dictating machine.
>
> By the time he arrives at work, there will be at least thirty or forty messages, memos, letters, and reminders to himself on the tape—some dictated enroute, some in a whisper in the middle of the night. The messages, when transcribed, will become part of Sweetheart Plastics' Executive VP George Shumrak's agenda for the day.

The next point deals with a newer context for dictation. But before getting into this interesting development, it is important to remember that despite advances in paperwork technology, older methods of dictation are likely to be around for a long time. These are:

•*The private secretary*—Even when the secretary is not so private (that is, services are shared by two or more executives) the status of having a secretary may be preferred by those whose standing in the organization gives them clout to get what they want. And some people, if they have the choice, prefer working with a secretary to using a machine.

•*The individual dictation setup*—Short of providing the full range of services inherent in effective word processing, a manager equipped with an individual dictating machine can get some of the advantages of mechanization. If, at the same time, a secretary or transcriptionist is located nearby to type the recorded words, the dictater may feel he or she has good control of the spoken-to-written word situation.

However, the wave of the future seems to favor the continuing advance of network word processing.

6. Effectiveness in Word-Processing Operations

A whole new dimension and importance has been added to the ability to dictate. Organizations that do word processing make dictation—the crucial *input* of the system—a qualification for, or at least a performance element of, many jobs. The better your input capability, that is, the better you can dictate, the more effective you will be in such a job.

In addition to these benefits, there is one less tangible but no less important. The person who dictates often can "write" better and faster. When you include an editing step, made especially easy by word-processing equipment, you can second-guess yourself to good advantage. The end result is likely to be a definite improvement over the handwritten or self-typed word.

Dictation as Input into a System

A final word about the importance of dictation as the input in word processing: several years ago I discussed my ideas about dictation with a top executive of a major manufacturer of dictation equipment. He believes that it is important to improve your ability to dictate:

> "Remember," he said, "the efficiency of any word-processing system is largely controlled by the input. This means, must mean, that the higher the effectiveness of the dictation, the better the entire system will work."

The implications of the statement are clear: the better you dictate, the better you fill your role as user and pacesetter of your organization's word processing.

Part I.
Dictation and You

2.
Learning Dictationese

Language, it has been said, is the human being's greatest invention. The intricate mental process by which we put ideas, feelings, and thoughts into words has made possible all our art and science, turned us into social beings who can form nations, build cities and travel to the moon.

The aim of this chapter is to help you master that particular kind of speech called dictation. I call it *dictationese* to identify it as a special language.

It must be said at the outset: A misconception about what dictation really is accounts for a large amount of the difficulty people have with dictating. There is a myth that is repeated endlessly, possibly with the best of intentions, but is, nevertheless, destructive. The myth is that dictation is just like talking. It's meant to minimize the nervousness of the would-be word originator. However, the mistaken impression the novice dictater has been given soon has its inhibiting effect. When the originator starts to dictate, he or she soon discovers that the process that should come so easily, doesn't. It is *not* just like talking.

I've been told by frustrated dictaters, "I have no trouble with ordinary conversation. Why can't I dictate better than I do?" You have to shatter the myth to get to the source of the trouble. The fact is, dictation isn't like anything else you do in terms of language.

The following points dispel the myth, and put word originators in a much stronger position to master the technique:

1. Dictation and Ordinary Speech Not the Same

•*Structure*—When you dictate, especially longer items, you usually have notes or an outline to help you pattern what you are saying. The result is a highly programmed activity, one in which you have no "freedom of speech" in the ordinary sense.

Regular talking is spontaneous; it doesn't require the preparation that characterizes good dictation. Ordinary talk proceeds with few, if any, restrictions. For example, you don't have to be concerned that a word, phrase, or even a whole thought, might be misunderstood. If you miss the intended mark, you can say to your listener, "Well, what I really mean is . . ." and, on the second round, carefully select the words that will convey your precise thought.

When you dictate, you don't have this latitude. You are speaking, literally, "for the record." And so you censor, refine as you go, knowing that your words will emerge in a permanent form. This is true even though you usually have the chance to correct and edit your copy.

•*Concentration*—"When I dictate," a participant in my dictation workshop said, "somehow it's different . . . not the same as a regular conversation." Examination of this "feeling" eventually isolated another quality unique to dictation. Unlike ordinary speech, dictation calls for a focused effort, concentration on the verbalizing taking place. Ordinary conversation usually takes place in a casual manner, with only minor expenditure of energy. But the bearing down, the sharp focus needed to make your thoughts and words stay on the dicta tion track, demand a degree of attention not needed when you're face to face with another person.

Implications of this fact are that, in the early learning phases, the dictater should be aware that mental and physical energies must be mobilized and applied to the process. When the person becomes experienced, the effort needed tapers off. The process of dictating becomes almost automatic, as is true of any well-learned task—driving a car, bike riding, dancing, and so on.

•*One-way communication*—When you dictate, the person or persons who are to receive your message are not present. Usually, when you speak, you are face-to-face with your listeners, or they are on the other end of a telephone. Communicating with someone you don't see or hear can make you feel awkward. It's a little like the first time you dial a friend's telephone number and, unexpectedly, are answered by a recorded message. Fortunately, it is not a major hurdle and, after a comparatively short period of practice, it is overcome.

Not seeing or hearing the person you are directing your message to also shapes the situation. In conversation, what you say is usually responded to by the listener. That response, in turn, may influence what your next utterance will be. When you dictate, the burden of developing a self-sufficient message rests entirely with you. What you say must be clear, logical, and understandable on its own terms.

•*Absense of body language*—In face-to-face conversation, a considerable part of your message is conveyed by your tone of voice, your body posture, your gestures, and your facial expression. None of these signals have any effect in dictation, especially when you are working with a recorder. This means that by your words, and your words alone, you must convey your message.

Of course, the flexibility and nuances of language make it possible to express both thoughts and feelings, whether simple or complex. People understand this dependence on words un-supported by body language.

Being aware of the reason for the difference between dic-tation and regular speech makes it possible for you to ap-proach dictation more realistically. In short, when you are new to dictation, any feeling that you are not in complete control is due to the fact that only part of your total equip-ment for communicating with others is being used. The non-verbal part—stance, gestures, and so on—cannot reinforce or round out your message. The accomplished dictater is able to surmount this lack, and make a message clear and effec-tive by words alone.

•*Need for instructions*—When you dictate, a certain amount of what you say is not aimed at the recipient of the message, but rather at the person who is typing the message. This means that the dictater must be prepared to interrupt his or her flow of words to give necessary instructions to the typist. This is a departure from normal expression and it takes get-ting used to. Listen to what a rapturous sentence sounds like when spoken in dictationese (the underlined words are meant for the transcriber):

Cap I love underline, you exclamation point.

This is another aspect of the special language word origi-nators must learn. When mastered, the language is easily spoken in a matter-of-fact manner.

2. Dictation Is Double-Talk

The better your mastery of dictation "double-talk—you are addressing two people, the recipient and the typist—the better your dictation skills are.

Your dictating situation, whether you are working with a secretary or a recording machine, partly determines the man-ner and amount of instructions you need to give. If you are working with a secretary who is familiar with your dictating needs and style, instructions may be minimal. The secretary knows from past experience how you want your letters punctuated. He or she is familiar with any special vocabulary you use because of the technical aspects of your business and knows the form in which you want your messages transcribed.

On the other hand, if you are dictating to a new secretary or using a word-processing system, your dictationese must feature instructions at every point where the typist cannot be expected to know what you want—the spelling of an unusual word, names and technical terms, and even the sign-off phrase with which you end the letter.

Figure 2-1 is an example of dictationese in action. Instructions to the transcriber are in all capital letters.

●*Learning the lingo*—Timothy E. McDonnelly's mastery of dictationese made it possible for him to get exactly the letter he had in mind. How about taking a crack at dictationese yourself? If you don't own a recorder, perhaps you can borrow one long enough to do these exercises.

Figure 2-2 is a memorandum from Mary Salinger, an administrative assistant in the Personnel Department. Working from the completed letter, can you give instructions to the typist as you dictate the communication, so that it will end up exactly as shown? Put yourself in the place of Mary Salinger. Using a tape recorder, speak the dictationese that will yield the desired result—the memorandum shown in Figure 2-2.

●*How to check your results*—Now that you've concluded the exercise, perhaps you can get a typist to transcribe your recording. Or put yourself in the role of transcriber. Play back the recording and think through the instruction part of your dictationese. Compare your memo with the one dictated by Mary Salinger. How closely does it match?

There are actually two checkpoints. In addition to matching the memorandum, the result of the dictationese, compare

(Text continued on page 16)

GOOD AFTERNOON OPERATOR, I'M TIMOTHY McDONNELLY IN THE EDITORIAL SERVICES DEPARTMENT. MY DICTATION IS FOR A MODIFIED BLOCK STYLE LETTER WITH MIXED PUNCTUATION AND INDENTED PARAGRAPHS. PLEASE TYPE FOR THE FINAL COPY ON OUR COMPANY LETTERHEAD. I'LL NEED ONE ORIGINAL AND THREE CARBONS. PLEASE FILE ONE IN CENTRAL RECORD'S STARCHILD FOLDER. DICTATION BEGINS. OPERATOR, PLEASE DATE THIS WITH TODAY'S DATE. THIS LETTER IS GOING TO Mr. Adam Starchild S-T-A-R-C-H-I-L-D NEXT LINE Starchild COMMA Incorporated NEXT LINE CAPITAL P PERIOD CAPITAL O PERIOD Box four three nine one NEXT LINE New York COMMA New York ZIP CODE one zero zero three five PARAGRAPH Dear Mr. Starchild COLON PARAGRAPH Your editor has informed me that you will compile the index for your forthcoming book COMMA OPERATOR, USE INITIAL CAPITALS FOR TITLE Tax Havens for Corporations PERIOD UNDERSCORE LAST FOUR WORDS As a professional indexer for Gulf Publishing Company COMMA I take this opportunity to offer you a few suggestions on preparing your index PERIOD PARAGRAPH You should begin by mentally placing yourself in the position of your reader PERIOD As you go through your page proofs COMMA pick out those items which are important and which you feel the reader might want to look for PERIOD Each item should be listed on a separate index card PERIOD PARAGRAPH Once you have selected an item for inclusion COMMA look for the key word which you can use as a guide for your referencing PERIOD How would the reader expect to find this item indexed QUESTION MARK PARAGRAPH For example COMMA if you want to index the phrase COMMA generation of commitment COMMA UNDERSCORE LAST THREE WORDS you would list it as commitment COMMA generation of UNDERSCORE LAST THREE WORDS because the reader would associate this phrase with the central idea of OPEN QUOTES commitment PERIOD CLOSE QUOTES However COMMA the phrase COMMA evaluation of employees COMMA UNDERSCORE LAST THREE WORDS would be listed under both evaluation UNDERSCORE LAST WORD and employees UNDERSCORE LAST WORD because the reader would logically look under either heading COMMA depending on his point of view PERIOD PARAGRAPH. Type your index on standard typing paper COMMA double HYPHEN spaced COMMA single column to a page COMMA then send it to us PERIOD Your editor will go through and make cross references you may have neglected to make and weed out any duplications PERIOD PARAGRAPH There are no hard and fast rules for deciding what should be included in an index PERIOD Try to keep your perspective and do not get carried away by the ideals of brevity or UNDERSCORE LAST WORD inclusiveness PERIOD PARAGRAPH Sincerely COMMA OPERATOR LEAVE THREE BLANK LINES Timothy E. McDonnelly OPERATOR PLEASE INCLUDE YOUR INITIALS. ADDRESS A STANDARD LETTER SIZE ENVELOPE. THANK YOU OPERATOR. THAT'S THE END OF THE DICTATION FOR THIS LETTER.

Figure 2-1. This exercise is an example of dictationese in action. Your dictation script above should produce a finished letter like the one shown on the right.

GULF PUBLISHING COMPANY

P. O. BOX 2608 ⌘ HOUSTON, TEXAS 77001 ✆ 713/529-4301

BOOK PUBLISHING DIVISION

(Current Date)

Mr. Adam Starchild
Starchild, Inc.
P. O. Box 4391
New York, NY 10035

Dear Mr. Starchild:

Your editor has informed me that you will compile the index for your forthcoming book, Tax Havens for Corporations. As a professional indexer for Gulf Publishing Company, I take this opportunity to offer you a few suggestions on preparing your index.

You should begin by mentally placing yourself in the position of your reader. As you go through your page proofs, pick out those items which are important and which you feel the reader might want to look for. Each item should be listed on a separate index card.

Once you have selected an item for inclusion, look for the key word which you can use as a guide for your referencing. How would the reader expect to find this item indexed?

For example, if you want to index the phrase, generation of commitment, you would list it as commitment, generation of because the reader would associate this phrase with the central idea of "commitment." However, the phrase, evaluation of employees, would be listed under both evaluation and employees because the reader would logically look under either heading, depending on his point of view.

Type your index on standard typing paper, double-spaced, single column to a page, then send it to us. Your editor will go through and make cross references you may have neglected to make and weed out any duplications.

There are no hard and fast rules for deciding what should be included in an index. Try to keep your perspective and do not get carried away by the ideals of brevity or inclusiveness.

Sincerely,

Timothy E. McDonnelly

pkc

Figure 2-1 (Continued).

your version of the dictationese with that of Mary Salinger. The more important comparison, however, is that of the end products. Wherever your version of the memo fails to coincide with Mary Salinger's, you can see how to correct the error by noting the instructions given in her dictationese. (See Figure 2-3.)

If you like, you may take another crack at the Mary Salinger memorandum. If you prefer, there is a second exercise on which to test your present skill.

In the second exercise, you are Bill Daniels of Administrative Services. You want to do a brief policy notice on the procedure for purchasing office supplies. Using a recorder, speak the dictationese that will get your typed copy exactly like that shown in Figure 2-4.

Compare your dictation with that of Bill Daniels. Daniels' dictationese and the typed copy are shown in Figure 2-5.

How close to Bill Daniels' dictationese did you come? Did you identify yourself and give your department affiliation? And how about spacing between lines and paragraphs?

The checklist shown in Figure 2-6 on page 22 will help you to further increase your understanding of dictationese. All the instruction elements in the dictationese you have read in the previous samples are simple words and phrases that soon become second nature to the dictater learning to speak the language. A list of the standard instructions can simplify the procedure. In cases where the dictater has a secretary or the transcriptionist is familiar with formats used, some of the instructions may be omitted.

3. Master Vocal Mechanics

Life can be easier for you and the transcriber if you remember a few things about voice control.

•*Speak distinctly*—Even if you are working with a secretary, this is good practice. If you are using a recorder, the lesser fi-

OFFICE MEMORANDUM

		Carbon Copies for:
Date	(Current Date)	
To	All Employees	
From	Mary Salinger, Personnel Dept.	
Subject	Office Security	

Certain persons are responsible for locking all doors to our offices at 4:45 p.m. Someone also has the responsibility of remaining in the offices during the noon hour. In the event this person has to leave at noon, you may be asked to remain in the offices to eat your lunch or to take a later lunch period.

Keys to the building are available for persons who need to work during weekends, holidays, or other times not regularly scheduled as working hours.

Be sure to lock your desk each night. If you do not have a key to your desk, notify the Department Head so that he or she can see about having one made.

The gate to the parking lot is locked promptly at 5:00 p.m. each evening. If you must work late, you should move your car to the front of the building or the parking lot west of the building.

We have floodlights which come on automatically at dark on the back parking lot, but at times these malfunction. If you are here after dark and notice that the floodlights are not on, please notify the Department Head.

Mary Salinger

pkc

Form 226

Figure 2-2. Test your dictationese. Give instructions that will produce a memorandum like the one shown.

delity of sound recording and playback make it difficult for the transcriber.

●*Don't distort the clarity of your voice*—Don't smoke, don't chew gum, and so on while dictating.

●*Use a conversational tone.*

GOOD MORNING OPERATOR, I'M MARY SALINGER IN THE PERSON-NEL DEPARTMENT. THIS PRIORITY TWO DOCUMENT IS A BLOCK STYLE MEMORANDUM TO BE TYPED FOR THE FINAL COPY ON COM-PANY MEMO FORM TWO TWENTY SIX. I'LL NEED ONE ORIGINAL AND ONE CARBON PLEASE. DICTATION FOLLOWS. OPERATOR, PLEASE DATE THIS MEMO WITH TODAY'S DATE. To all employees from Mary Sal-inger COMMA INITIAL CAPITALS FOR NEXT TWO WORDS Personnel De-partment Subject Office Security PARAGRAPH TRIPLE SPACE Certain per-sons are responsible for locking all doors to our offices at ARABIC NU-MERALS four COLON four five SMALL P PERIOD SMALL M PERIOD Some-one also has the responsibility of remaining in the offices during the noon hour PERIOD In the event this person has to leave at noon COMMA you may be asked to remain in the offices to eat your lunch or to take a later lunch period PERIOD PARAGRAPH Keys to the building are available for persons who need to work during weekends COMMA holidays COMMA or other times not regularly scheduled as working hours PERIOD PARAGRAPH Be sure to lock your desk each night PERIOD If you do not have a key to your desk COMMA notify the INITIAL CAPITALS FOR THE NEXT TWO WORDS Department Head so that he or she can see about having one made PERIOD PARA-GRAPH The gate to the parking lot is locked promptly at ARABIC NU-MERALS five COLON zero zero SMALL P PERIOD SMALL M PERIOD each evening PERIOD If you must work late COMMA you should move your car to the front of the building or the parking lot west of the building PERIOD PARA-GRAPH We have floodlights which come on automatically at dark on the back parking lot COMMA but at times these malfunction PERIOD If you are here after dark and notice that the floodlights are not on COMMA please notify the INITIAL CAPITALS FOR THE NEXT TWO WORDS Department Head PE-RIOD PARAGRAPH OPERATOR, THAT COMPLETES THE DICTATION FOR THIS MEMORANDUM. PLEASE PUT YOUR INITIALS AT THE LOWER LEFT CORNER. THANK YOU.

Figure 2-3. This is the dictationese Mary Salinger used to get the finished memorandum in Figure 2-2. Compare your memo to hers, and correct any error by noting the instructions she used.

• *Use voice modulation to differentiate between the message and instructions*—A change of tone can alert the typist to punctuation—commas and periods, for example. You also verbally indicate the punctuation: "And so, comma, after all this time, comma, we still are not sure where we stand period."

Policy Sheet # 17

PURCHASE ORDERS AND SUPPLIES

Normal office supplies (pens, pencils, paper, paper clips, etc.) are stocked in the supply cabinets here in our offices and are readily available to you. However, should you take the last pencil, box of paper clips, or whatever, please notify the person who does the ordering so that the stock may be replenished immediately. Many other items not stocked here in these offices are available through the Mailroom. Should you require any nonconsumable or consumable item not normally stocked by the company, please do not order it directly or through the Mailroom until you have a purchase order made out and authorized by the Department Head.

The purchase order number should be given to the supplier so that it will be on the invoice when it arrives.

The carbon of the purchase order will be returned to you when it is signed and you should keep this until the invoice comes in. At that time, the invoice will be forwarded to you and you should attach the carbon of the purchase order to the invoice.

We use (3) classfications of purchase order numbers. Those preceded with an "SD" are for the Sales Department, those with an "AD" are for the Accounting Department, and those with a "CD" are for the Circulation Department. Thus, when an invoice comes in with, say, SD-147 on it, we know it should go to the Sales Department for approval.

Figure 2-4. Another exercise in dictationese. Try to give instructions that will yield the page shown here.

●*Avoid social chat that may be interpreted as part of your message*—For example, a department head was surprised to get back a letter that read: "Just got the production figures for last week, I've got to get out to lunch in the next fifteen minutes, and they sure look good . . ."

●*Try to maintain a steady pace and a uniform voice level*—If you talk loudly at one point, and your voice drops at another, the typist may not be able to catch the lower range, no matter how the volume control on the playback instrument is regulated. An uneven pace tends to throw a transcriber off.

People who have regional or foreign accents sometimes run into trouble with machine transcription. It will help if your typing can be done by a person less likely to be floored by an unusual delivery.

4. Another Secret: Personalize

"To whom am I speaking?" One of the participants in the dictation workshop raised this unexpected question. At first her query was not understood. She explained: "When I dictate to a stenographer, I am not really talking to her. And when I use a recording machine, I'm not talking to myself. Then, who am I talking to?"

The question may sound simple or even incongruous. But the fact is it's more profound and the answer more useful than one might think. It is important that you do speak to someone. That person may or may not be a real individual. Here are two possibilities:

●*An actual person*—When you're dictating a letter to John Smith or a memo to Mary Jones, it helps to visualize them as you speak. The message tends to become more of an actual exchange, more clearly directed toward the person.

Even if you don't know the recipient (it may be a letter to a person you've never met, a memo to a newcomer in the or-

OPERATOR, THIS IS BILL DANIELS IN THE ADMINISTRATIVE SERVICES DEPARTMENT. IF YOU HAVE ANY QUESTIONS ABOUT THIS UNBOUND MANUSCRIPT, PLEASE CALL ME AT EXTENSION TWO NINE ONE. I'LL NEED JUST ONE ORIGINAL ON PLAIN WHITE BOND PAPER SUITABLE FOR PHOTOCOPYING. INDENT ALL PARAGRAPHS AND SINGLE SPACE THE BODY ON THIS MANUSCRIPT. DICTATION BEGINS. IN THE UPPER LEFT CORNER OF THE PAGE PLEASE TYPE WITH INITIAL CAPITALS AND UNDERSCORE THE NOTICE Policy Sheet NUMBER SIGN Number ARABIC NUMERALS one seven. PLEASE TRIPLE SPACE AND CENTER THE TITLE IN ALL CAPITALS, Purchase Orders and Supplies. TRIPLE SPACE PARAGRAPH Normal office supplies OPEN PAREN pens COMMA pencils COMMA paper COMMA paper clips COMMA et cetera CLOSE PAREN are stocked in the supply cabinets here in our offices and are readily available to you PERIOD However COMMA should you take the last pencil COMMA box of paper clips COMMA or whatever COMMA please notify the person who does the ordering so that the stock may be replenished immediately PERIOD Many other items not stocked here in these offices are available through the INITIAL CAPITAL Mailroom PERIOD Should you require any nonconsumable or consumable item not normally stocked by the company COMMA please do not order it directly or through the Mailroom until you have a purchase order made out and authorized by the INITIAL CAPITALS Department Head PERIOD PARAGRAPH The purchase order number should be given to the supplier so that it will be on the invoice when it arrives PERIOD PARAGRAPH The carbon of the purchase order will be returned to you when it is signed and you should keep this until the invoice comes in PERIOD At that time COMMA the invoice will be forwarded to you and you should attach the carbon of the purchase order to the invoice PERIOD PARAGRAPH We use OPEN PAREN ARABIC NUMERAL three CLOSE PAREN classifications of purchase order numbers PERIOD Those preceded with an OPEN QUOTES CAP S CAP D CLOSE QUOTES are for the INITIAL CAPITALS ON NEXT TWO WORDS Sales Department COMMA those with an OPEN QUOTES CAP A CAP D CLOSE QUOTES are for the INITIAL CAPITALS Accounting Department COMMA and those with a OPEN QUOTES CAP C CAP D CLOSE QUOTES are for the INITIAL CAPITALS Circulation Department PERIOD Thus COMMA when an invoice comes in with COMMA say COMMA CAP S CAP D HYPHEN ARABIC NUMERALS one four seven on it COMMA we know it should go to the INITIAL CAPITALS ON THE NEXT TWO WORDS Sales Department for approval PERIOD. OPERATOR, THAT COMPLETES THE DICTATION ON THIS NOTICE. THANK YOU.

Figure 2-5. This is the dictationese that Bill Daniels used in dictating the page shown in Figure 2-4. If your page differs from his, compare your dictationese to his instructions.

Instruction Checklist for Word Originators

Before You Begin

1. Identify yourself
2. Indicate type of dictation:
    Letter
    Memo
    Report
    Other
3. Rough draft? Hold job?
4. Kind of paper or letterhead
5. Secretarial instructions—format, spacing, etc.
6. Name and address—spell

During Your Dictation

1. Unusual punctuation
2. Secretarial instructions:
    Spelling—technical/unusual words
    Single/double spacing change
    Underscoring
    Special punctuation
    Indentations
    Paragraph
3. Special instruction(s)—forgotten or out-of-sequence instructions

After

1. Signature
2. Names of persons receiving carbon copies (spell)
3. Enclosures
4. End dictation

Figure 2-6. This checklist for word originators will help you understand dictationese. These instructions are to be given before, during, and after your dictation.

ganization), it is still possible to develop an image of a person, starting with the name, the organization to which the individual belongs, a title and so on. These images may be stereotypes, but they make you feel that there is a person out there with whom you are communicating.

•*Typical representative of a group*—One top business editor, when instructing newcomers to his staff, says, "When you write to our audience, keep in mind the president of the Unique Plastic Company, a small- to middle-size organization located in Chicago . . ."

Some people find it a great deal easier to dictate to an individual, real or hypothetical. They find that with this person in mind they are better able to slant the copy the way they want it to go because they understand the audience's attitudes, evaluations, and level of intelligence. Even the vocabulary level used is determined by the capabilities of the person in their mind's eye.

Part I.
Dictation and You

3.
Word Processing: Challenge and Opportunity

Dictation was used in the ancient world. The people who could not write, or those who couldn't be bothered, had scribes record their messages. Eventually dictation-by-necessity was replaced by dictation for the sake of efficiency.

Dictation took a giant leap forward when typewriters became standard office equipment. Systems of shorthand were developed to minimize the difference between the speed of the spoken word and the rate at which the words could be recorded.

The executive-secretary team multiplied by several times the efficiency of earlier means of business communication. The invention of the typewriter—mass-produced models became available at the turn of the century—came at a time when the business world was bursting with growth. New industries, from paint to automobiles, appeared. There was a need for extensive communication. Executives with improved dictating ability, and the secretary's improved stenographic and typing skills, aided by electrification of the typewriter, speeded the exchange of information.

Paperwork Technology Surges Ahead

The dictating executive and the capable steno-typist secretary made an effective team. Relieved of the direct burden of producing the written word, the dictater was able to apply the time saved to other matters. Figure 3-1 shows how the team looked schematically.

In the 1880s Thomas Edison invented the phonograph and predicted its use in turning out correspondence. It was the sound recorder that led to the next turn of the wheel in business communication—the individual dictating transcriber unit. With this equipment, the dictater committed to tape, belt, or disc, letters and office memos. The dictation recording was then played back on a compatible machine from which a typist converted the spoken message directly into a typed one. (See Figure 3-2.)

The next step in word processing was the development of the typing pool. The usual procedure was for managers to record their communications and send the tape or belt to a unit which provided transcription services. (See Figure 3-3.)

With the creation of typing pools, major changes were in store both for word processing and the organization. Some of the consequences included:

1. The traditional executive/secretary team became less common. Usually, only higher-echelon executives required secretaries.
2. With the steno-typing element removed from most secretaries' duties, they were able to undertake more responsibility, and became—often with the title—administrative assistants.
3. While some secretaries entered the typing pool, organizations began recruiting a new and specialized type of office worker, the transcriber-typist.

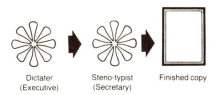

Figure 3-1. A schematic view of the executive-secretary team, the first step in the advancement of word processing technology.

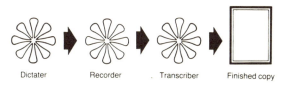

Figure 3-2. The invention of the sound recorder made the transfer of information easier. The executive (dictater) recorded the message and passed the tape to the transcriber (typist) who produced finished copy.

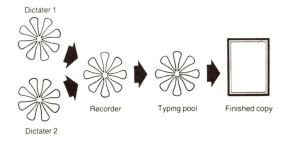

Figure 3-3. This shows the next step in word processing—the typing pool. Executives would dictate their memos, send the tape to the typing pool, and receive finished copy from the typists.

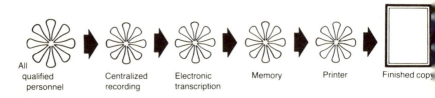

All
qualified   Centralized   Electronic   Memory   Printer   Finished copy
personnel   recording   transcription

Figure 3-4. This schematic reflects today's basic word processing system. Electronic transcription units hooked up to a computer-controlled memory and printer have replaced the conventional typewriter in many offices.

4. Non-executive personnel (technicians, supervisors), traditionally without benefit of secretarial help, could now take advantage of the typing pool as an assist in their written communications.

Once the typing pool appeared, equipment manufacturers developed machines that would increase the efficiency of the system. Building on the centralization of the typing operation, equipment was devised that made it possible to dictate directly into recorders located near the typists.

Soon, typists were no longer limited to typing on paper, with all the hazards of typographical errors as well as those committed by the dictaters. Keyboards were hooked up to a CRT element, a cathode-ray tube on which the typed message was displayed. The message was recorded on a computer-controlled medium so that corrections could be made, either during the typing or after a first draft had been printed. The draft was sent back to the dictater, corrected by him or her, then returned to the center where changes were made on the stored message, which was then printed in final form. (See Figure 3-4.)

If the first draft of a message was correct, the basic system was sufficient. But if the dictater made changes, additional steps were required. (See Figure 3-5.) Note that the basic system doesn't change, merely that a correction step is added at the transcriber-CRT unit.

Operator of transcriber/CRT unit brings item to be corrected back from memory unit   Memory unit incorporates corrections   Printer   Finished final copy

Figure 3-5. A correction step added to the basic word processing system allows the dictater to easily correct errors in the original copy.

The word-processing bandwagon is rolling along at an accelerating rate. Executives of all kinds—business, government, institutional—are staying awake nights deciding whether or not to jump aboard and replace present paperwork methods with word-processing equipment. Those who have acquired simple systems are wondering whether they should now install more recent sophisticated models. And those involved in supplying word-processing hardware (manufacturers of machines, from recorders to automatic printers) are trying to anticipate marketing needs, and get a jump on the competition.

The Push Behind Word Processing

There is no mystery as to the factors that keep the word-processing pot boiling. They are the same as those that explain technological progress ever since the industrial revolution:

•*Cost saving*—Organizations with WP equipment that has been acquired after a careful survey of needs generally report favorably on new operating costs vs. old. A typical savings figure is 20 percent, although some are higher. One study of the cost of a business letter contrasted the dictater-secretary team ($4.47) and the dictater-dictation machine ($3.51)—a 21 percent saving. Salaries of the dictater and secretary accounted for more than half of the letter's total cost. In cases where expected WP savings fail to materialize, management usually admits that there has been a failure to implement original plans.

•*Time saving*—One equipment manufacturer explains the savings in this way: "Dictation doesn't dominate the time of two people when only one is needed for the job." In other words, dictating to a recording machine is a one-person job as opposed to the executive-secretary team.

Other figures also support the time-saving factor. For example, the average speed of machine dictation is sixty words per minute, which is three times the productivity of handwriting, and twice that of face-to-face dictation. That means the dictater—often a time-starved executive—benefits from machine vs. steno use.

•*Convenience*—Dictation equipment is ready to work whenever the word originator is. In practical terms, this means that there need be no delay while a dictater waits for his or her secretary to return from lunch. Or, the dictater may come in before regular starting hours, or stay after hours, without requiring the special cooperation of a secretary.

•*Mobility*—Hand-held, battery-operated recorders may be used in the field or at home, while traveling or in a hotel room. The side benefit of out-of-office use of hand-held units is that they leave office time for other work.

•*Improved quality*—Fast, inexpensive, and sophisticated WP equipment makes completely error-free typing possible. The old office rule of, "No correspondence goes outside with more than two erasures," is obsolete. Attempts at concealing typos by whiting out, for example, are usually obvious, unesthetic, and suggest sloppy operation—unfavorable to any organization's image.

•*High-level skill shortage*—"A good all-around secretary is practically impossible to find," reports a recruiter for an employment agency that specializes in office help. And he adds, the salary expectations of those who qualify are very high.

Despite the proliferation of centralized or network systems, the individual dictation machine is still widely used. There is some controversy in professional circles as to the future of the individual machine. Many feel that network word processing is the wave of the future.

For practical reasons, however, it seems likely that both approaches will continue to grow in use. Small companies usually do not need and cannot afford a sophisticated network system. For the larger organization, the appeal of the network system lies in its capacity. Individuals who need to dictate only occasionally can have access to typing assistance when it is needed.

Experiences with WP—A Cautionary Tale

In the course of research into WP installations and practices, I came upon two companies, both with well-designed WP systems. But, their experiences with the units were quite different.

•*Company A*—This is a large insurance company with 150 potential word originators. Almost all make use of the WP unit. And each originator is given a personal briefing by the WP supervisor, using an informal but thorough approach:

> "I know a lot of people are afraid of the equipment at first," she says. "So when I demonstrate machine use, I make mistakes, point them out, and show how corrections are made. This reduces the worry a good deal."

This supervisor also keeps track of the percentage of pieces dictated by each originator that must be returned for correction.

> "This record is in no way used to pressure people to strive for perfect copy. Instead of helping, that would be a handicap. Some people would just stop using our services. When I see an originator with a consistently high return rate—and it can go over

100 percent if items are returned more than once—I check with him or her to see what's wrong. About half the time it's poor dictation. The other half is faulty use of the equipment, or not knowing our procedures."

This WP unit has bettered original projections in terms of service objectives and costs. "Our turnaround time is down to one or two hours," the supervisor says. This is the time elapsing between dictation and the arrival of the copy back at the originator's office. Management estimates that paperwork handled by the WP department is costing the company 25 percent less and the service is available to many more people, including technicians and other professionals who ordinarily would not have regular secretarial help available to them.

•*Company B*—This is the home office of a large bank. The supervisor of the WP unit is as intelligent and capable as his opposite number in Company A. But he has problems:

"Only about 30 percent of those who could use our service do. And we're in a vicious circle. I don't get the cooperation I'd like to have from my authors, and that slows us down. Our turnaround time is half a day at the very best, and sometimes two or three days. Then, because we seem to be so slow, people have a good argument for not using us."

The equipment in companies A and B is similar. The difference seems largely a matter of top management resolve and interest. In Company A, management has given the WP unit full backing. Anything that can be handled by the service is expected to be worked through it. In Company B, a large percentage of originators are top executives who resist the idea of giving up their private secretaries. To justify this stance, inconveniences real and imagined are attributed to the WP unit. The result, as the supervisor sees it, is that . . . "Since I have no clout in the organization—certainly not in confrontation with executives—I am very limited in what I can do to improve our service."

It seems unlikely that any contemplated cost saving has actually been made in Company B's installation.

For policy makers, the comparison between Company A and Company B suggests a caution: Don't opt for an expensive WP system if negative attitudes and resistance are going to interfere with the system's use. Prepare your people. Educate and proselytize until you get acceptance. Make the actual installation start-ups as trouble-free as possible.

For dictaters, especially those whose organization has some version of a centralized system: It's up to you to use the system to your best advantage. This will also benefit the WP department. Accordingly, you can score improvement for both yourself and the service unit.

Making the System Work for You

In order to optimize your use of a word-processing unit, it's desirable that you develop a symbiotic relationship with it. In this mutually advantageous situation, both you and the unit develop the practices that lead to mutual benefit.

You achieve this desirable goal by observing certain guidelines.

1. Dealing with People

The impression some visitors have of a department is that a WP area is made up largely of expensive and highly technical machines and faceless individuals. It's easy to lose sight of the fact that a word-processing unit consists of a number of people working with a number of machines.

But as a user of the unit, remember that it is the people who operate the machines with whom you deal. And so your relationships should be the same as with any other departmental group—one of mutual help and cooperation, with human values enhancing procedures.

The supervisor of the unit is the person with whom you the primary point of contact, the one who can make suggestions that will help you operate better, and who can help you solve problems if your dictation is of an unroutine kind. Then, there are the other individuals in the department, the machine operators or other assistants, whose skills and morale can make or break the efficiency of the entire setup. Keep in mind that no matter how mechanical the contact (for example, you may be sending a cassette through the mail to be transcribed, or dictating on your telephone to a centralized tape-recording system), there will be a person at the other end of the line. Their success in transcribing your work depends heavily on the quality of the material you send. In general, a transcriber will not have the same opportunities to verify information (the spelling of unusual names, formats, and so on) that the conventional secretary has. Keep in mind the transcriber's human limitations and ask yourself: Could I translate these words and instructions if *I* were at the receiving end?

2. Learn WP Unit Procedures

No WP systems are alike. Even if the equipment is the same in two units, it's likely that procedures differ.

If you are new to the organization, or if the WP system is new, take advantage of any orientation program that the unit supervisor offers. Learn the correct methods recommended for the word originators. Also, develop an overall picture of the sequence of operations, not only what the equipment can do, but what it can't or won't do as limited by procedures.

The efficiency of WP requires specific systems designed to meet the needs of a number of different authors. While most units try to be flexible, standard ways of handling work help maintain efficiency. Ask the supervisor about specific rules if you are in doubt. And as far as possible, submit work that is in line with the requirements.

3. Make Operation of Equipment Second Nature

There is a wide range of input equipment. For example, you may have an individual recording machine on your desk. It may use tape, discs, or some other medium. Or your organization may have a centralized system to which you have access by your regular telephone. Whatever the nature of the equipment you use, learn to operate it well enough so as not to have to think about it as you go through the various phases of dictation.

If the equipment is new to you, be sure to get operating instructions. A demonstration can be most helpful, whether it is given to you by the WP supervisor or the company supplying the equipment.

Some supervisors suggest that you experiment with the equipment for a while to understand what it can do and how it performs its function. Undertake a few test runs with the new equipment. Ask your WP unit to go along with your test, either having the material transcribed or just having it checked over by the supervisor. Get his or her comments as to how well it suits the transcriber's needs.

As you gain experience by using the equipment regularly, your familiarity and mastery of it will increase. With each use you gain know-how. Practice the routine that gives you trouble—it may be making corrections, for example, or giving the operator sufficient direction. Whatever your weak points, give them special attention so that they cease being factors that contribute to inefficiency.

4. Learn How WP Unit Can Help You

From time to time, the WP operation may change, usually by way of improving its capacity or the sophistication of its operation. When such improvements are made, be sure you understand them well enough to use them. Informal talks with the supervisor or with other people in the unit can help you fill out the picture of WP capabilities.

One WP supervisor I interviewed said that she made it a point to remind authors of WP capabilities that were not used as often as they might be. "There were a group of authors," she explained, "who didn't understand how corrections could be made during dictation. I set up meetings with them in which I demonstrated just how the equipment could be used. It made their dictation easier for them and easier for us as well."

If you are in doubt about any aspect of the capabilities of the WP unit, ask the WP supervisor if you can see a demonstration of the equipment. Again, learn the capabilities and the limitations of the system in terms of the work you are sending to be processed.

Further, discuss special projects with WP personnel. Whenever possible give advance warning on a big job or one that has high priority. One supervisor advises: "If you constantly get work back with the same errors, bring it to my attention. Or, if authors are unsure as to how to handle a particular item, it's best to ask for assistance in advance. This will help us handle the job more easily."

5. Know How You Can Help WP People

The more closely you follow established procedures, the better you will be cooperating with the people who run the unit. If in doubt about any procedure, it's wise to clear up your questions in advance.

Remember, every word originator represents input into the system. This input is a major factor in the overall effectiveness of the WP unit.

By taking advantage of any special services, you increase the level of your cooperation. Whenever you have a job that might be handled by WP, check with the unit before going to another source. Even if you think the job is outside WP's capabilities, the people in the WP unit usually will welcome the challenge of new and different work. As one WP department head says, "It gives us a chance to show how good we are."

6. Keep In Touch

Word-processing units tend to change from time to time. One reason for the changes is that new and more sophisticated equipment may be acquired. Another reason is to bring services more in line with word originators' needs.

A head of a WP unit I visited suggests: "Word originators should set up appointments for informal visits from time to time. Particularly if there are new developments, the WP unit is worth a visit. A walk around and a demonstration of equipment can give you a much clearer view of the services that can be rendered."

Because they are occasionally the forgotten people in the organization, any compliments or kind words you can send along to WP personnel will be happily received.

A supervisor says, "I make a special point of trying to improve relations between word originators and my people. One way I do this is to encourage the transcribers to phone authors and discuss any problems or questions that arise. And when things slow down, it's not unusual for transcribers to call an author and make any helpful comments they may have about the dictation they have been working on."

Keeping in touch also includes letting WP personnel in on any problems you may have at your end or with the copy you're getting back. The WP people can't work on problems they don't know about. When you bring difficulties to their attention—generally going through the supervisor first—you make it possible for them to come up with solutions that can make your life and theirs a bit easier.

Word Processing Terminology

Author, dictator, or word originator—the person who provides the input (words) to be converted to a written message

Automated typewriters—typewriters that can store information, then print it when instructed to do so

Automatic forward reset—a central telephone dictation recorder feature that automatically locks in the playback mode to the end of the dictation

Automatic gain control—regulates volume for dictation and transcription

Automatic recall—a machine feature to replay the last few words automatically at each start

Automatic reverse—a tape reaches the end, it will automatically reverse and playback

Automatic selector—an electronic switching device on the dictation system which automatically directs dictation to a recorder that is not being used

Automatic terminals—a computer system capable of producing and editing documents

Backlog—the number of dictated documents to be processed

Block style—all lines in a letter begin flush with the left margin

Camera-ready—a document prepared for reproduction by photography

Carbon set—thin paper with carbon sheets attached

Cartridge—a container holding a magnetic medium

Cassette—a roll of magnetic tape housed in a rectangular case

Cathode-ray tube (CRT)—a vacuum tube which displays key-boarded characters

CT/ST—cassette tape/selectric typewriter

CPU—central processing unit

Centralized system—a central recorder and transcription station which receives dictation from various locations

Clipped—a word or word part not recorded because dictation began before the record mode was actuated

Close punctuation—punctuation marks after all principal letter parts

Combination unit—a single unit designed for both dictation and transcription

Compatibility—the ability of various units to function together

Continuous or endless loop—an endless tape, permanently sealed in a tank for dictation and transcription

Correction feature—allows a typist to backspace and type in the correct characters

Cue—an electronic signal introduced on the magnetic tape

DE—dictating equipment

Decibel—a unit of measure for the relative intensity of sound

Dedicated unit—a dictation unit for one person or a specific type of document

Degaussing—the process of demagnetizing

Desk-top-unit—a self-contained dictation or transcription unit designed for individual use

Dial access—ability to dial a certain telephone number to control a dictation unit

Distortion—an inaccurate reproduction of a signal

Distribution—document delivery

Draft—rough copy of a document

Dropout—words not heard during playback

Dynamic microphone—an electromagnetic pressure instrument for transmitting sounds

Edit—make corrections, additions, and/or deletions to a document

Element—a spherical typing font

Elite type—twelve spaces of type per horizontal inch

Error-free capability—the ability to dictate over errors

Facsimile—a machine that transmits and receives a picture of a document by using telephone lines

Fast forward—used to advance a recording at a high speed

Fidelity—the degree of accurate sound reproduction

Final copy—perfected document

Floppy disc—recording storage medium

Flutter—pitch and volume distortions

Font—a set of one size and style of type

Format decision—determining how a document should be arranged on a page

Galley proof—a preliminary printed document

Gap—the distance between the poles of a magnetic recorder head

Handset—hand-held transmitter and receiver for dictation

Hard copy—a typewritten document

Hardware—the physical components of an equipment system

Hertz (HZ)—cycles per second

Image—the impression made on paper

Ips—inches per second

Indent—to space in from a margin

Indented paragraphs—the first line of each paragraph spaced inward five to ten spaces from the margin

Infocom—shared computer system for transmitting information

Input unit—dictation equipment

Inverted paragraph style—the first line of each paragraph begins at the left margin and the following lines of the paragraph are indented five spaces

Justify—to make lines of type a specific length

Keyboarding—to enter information on an electronic keyboard

Light emitting diodes (LED)—an electronic index-display system which eliminates the need for paper index strips or discs

Logic—programmed instructions to equipment

Lower case—small letters; not capitals

MC/ST—Mag Card Selectric Typewriter

Magnetic media typewriter—a typewriter with a magnetic medium designed to record and print keyboarded information

MT/SC—Magnetic Tape Selectric Composer

MT/ST—Magnetic Tape Selectric Typewriter

Management duties/word processing duties—separation of the work load so that some secretaries do general typing while others assist in specific administrative functions

Manual selector—a switch at the dictation station to allow the originator to select a recorder

Media—materials on which recordings are made

Memory—a feature to record, store, and play back information

Merge—to combine or consolidate two or more parts of document

Microfiche—a plastic card containing strips of greatly reduced document photographs

Microfilm—a fine grained film with extremely small document photographs

Microprocessor—a computer-like unit inside a word processor that performs the sensing, communications, and control functions

Mil—one-thousandth of an inch (indicates tape thickness)

Minicomputer—a small computer with limited functions

Mixed or standard punctuation—indicates to use a colon after the salutation and a comma after the complimentary close

Mode—operating condition of a machine

Modified block—a letter's style with the date and complimentary close at the horizontal center

Modified block style—the dateline and closing begin at the center while other letter parts begin at the left margin

Module—an interchangeable component

Multiple-part forms—duplicated pages bound together under the top sheet

Off-line—independent from a central processor

On-line—Connected to a central processor

Open punctuation—no punctuation used after the salutation or complimentary close

Output unit—equipment used to produce a typewritten document

Paper tape—a recording medium in some editing typewriters

Patch—to transfer recorded material to another medium

Pause control—a dictation unit feature on the microphone or handset to stop and start the tape

Photoelectric reader—an electronic reader device on some automated typewriters

Pica type—ten characters per horizontal inch

Playback—the process of listening to the dictation

Portable unit—a small self-contained battery-operated dictation unit

Power keyboard—refers to the keyboard on automated typewriters

Power typing—rapid typing on an automated typewriter

Printer—the unit used to actually type the document

Privacy lock-out—prevents other originators from erasing or listening to the dictation of others

PBX dictation system—a centralized dictation system using dial or touch-tone telephones

Private wire—a centralized dictation system not wired to the telephone company's lines

Ready tone—a tone indicating a recorder is available for dictation

Recall—to bring information back from storage for listening or typing

Reel-to-reel—a recorder which does not use cassettes or cartridges

Reference code—an electronic indexing signal made on magnetic tape

Scan—listening to a tape at an accelerated rate to locate a specific part of the dictation

Shared logic—various units share a centralized computer's logic system

Simplified style—a basic block style letter without salutation and complimentary close

Strikeover—when one character is typed over another

Software—a program describing equipment operation

Sound sheet—a flat vinyl recording medium

Squeal—a noise resulting from the stick and release of a tape

Stat typing—top priority typing

Talk-down tone—a tone to remind originators to talk louder

Telecopier—equipment used to transmit pictures of documents over telephone lines

Telephone message coupler (TMC)—an interface device to connect dictating equipment to telephone lines

Teletypewriter—a unit which sends and receives information over lines

Text editor—a typewriter that edits, manipulates, and alters text

Tone control—used to vary the treble and base tones in playback

Track—the path on which a channel of sound is recorded

Transcription—the process of typing dictated material

Trunk—a telephone line

Turnaround time—the time from dictation to final copy

Unattended recorder—an automatic recorder with the capability to accept dictation without an operator's presence

Unload—to remove a tape belt or cartridge from a unit

Upper case—signifies capital letters

Voice guard—a tone to warn the originator that the media is not moving

VOR—voice operated relay

Word processing (WP)—a systematic organization of people, equipment and procedures to transfer information from a verbal to a written form

Part II.
Three Ways to Prepare

4.
Setting the Preliminaries

In talking with people who dictate, it often turns out that a major problem is insufficient preparation. While this may not be the case for you, a rundown of major preliminaries can help even experienced dictaters review their practices and possibly strengthen a weak point or two.

Master the Procedure

Whether you work with a secretary or a machine, there are certain procedures that you and the secretary and/or the word-processing people should agree to and understand.

If you have a secretary, the procedures involving dictation and transcription are usually simple and readily agreed to because physical proximity makes ongoing communication possible. For example:

Executive Bill Gridley has started dictation when his boss comes in for an unexpected quickie conference. Gridley says, "Marion, type out your notes as far as we've gone and we'll pick up a little later."

Procedures for working with a secretary should include specifics involving everything from how you want your correspondence filed to when the best times for dictation will be. However, procedures involving a dictater and a word-processing unit involve somewhat more detail. For example, the time a message is dictated may have to be carefully worked out so that an important letter can be transcribed, edited, retyped, and ready for the last mail of the day.

Some procedural elements that require mutual agreement between dictater and secretary or WP unit are:

●*Time and timing*—A letter you dictate at 4 p.m. may not be able to make the last batch of outgoing mail. Have an understanding on last-mail deadlines.

In the event that you have an urgent letter that *must* go out, make special arrangements such as overtime for the typist and someone who will get the letter satisfactorily posted.

The matter of timing should not be viewed as troublesome. On the contrary, secretaries and WP supervisors appreciate a dictater's thoughtfulness when an urgent job can be done without a last-minute frenzy. Similarly, a dictater is pleased when a secretary or WP employee takes special pains with a difficult piece of dictation.

●*Style*—You should not have to detail the format of every message. Consult with the person who does your typing, and agree on three or four standard formats that will do for most letters and memos.

If this agreement is followed by samples of the specified typing styles, your instruction can be as simple as, "Use letter style No. 1."

●*Nomenclature*—Be sure that your typist understands instruction words or those used fairly regularly in the body of your text. Words like *delete*, *all caps*, *underscores* are simple and specific as long as the transcriber knows their meaning. If not, a brief consultation can make up for this unfamiliarity.

Technical terms within the text can cause problems if the typist is new in the organization. When in doubt, spell out the term or explain it in the course of your dictation. To prevent misspellings, one thoughtful manager sent the WP supervisor a list of 25 words that constituted industry-wide jargon.

•*Watch out for sound-alikes (homophones)*—Some transcriptions that have amused, horrified or irritated authors include: *ceiling wax* instead of *sealing wax*; *double day* instead of *Doubleday*; *urgent male* instead of *urgent mail*; and *pears to me* instead of *appears to me*. The list goes on and on, and you may add those from your own experience. Obviously, the rule in the case of sound-alike words is to spell out the one you are using.

The procedures you are involved in must become part of your working and dictating style. The simpler the procedures are and the better they fit into your overall schedule, the more effective you will become.

In almost every case, it pays to review how you've been doing in your dictating procedures. If there are any inconveniences, delays, logjams, or obstacles, make the business of eliminating them a joint venture between you and your secretary or you and the unit supervisor.

How to Give Instructions

Dictationese, as described earlier, requires that you use "doubletalk" because you are directing thoughts to both the transcriber and the recipient of the message. It's essential that the typist be able to differentiate between the message and instructions.

•*Signal your instructions*—You can convey the information in two ways: First, modulate your voice so that instructions are given in a somewhat crisper and more direct tone than the body of the message; and second, a device used by some experienced dictaters is to say the typist's name. For example: ". . . and at your earliest convenience period. Helen, the sentences that follow should be set to a margin about an inch indent on both sides." The typist knows that when her name is used instructions, not text, will follow it. If you're recording and do not know the name of the typist, the designation *operator* may be used.

•*Spacing*—If you're certain that the message, being short and uncomplicated, will require no second draft, you may specify single spacing. On the other hand, if you expect to do some editing so that your dictation represents a first draft on which you may strike out words, add new ones, delete sentences and so on, it helps to follow the practice used by professional writers which is to double-space the copy. If you expect the editing to be heavy, triple spacing may be desirable. The presumption is that on the retype you will ask for the line spacing that you want on the final draft.

•*Typographical errors*—It's advisable to instruct your typist not to strive for perfect copy when you expect to do some editing. This doesn't mean messy typing, but since you're going to be marking up the copy, you don't want to waste the typist's time by having typos corrected. Other imperfections in first draft typing—faulty margins, incorrect paragraphing—can be remedied in the retype.

Your Best Physical Setup

Some people can work efficiently standing on one leg, surrounded by noisy activities of all kinds—telephones ringing, people shouting, etc. They are the exceptions. For the most part, the more you can do to increase the comfort and convenience of your situation, the better.

•*Reasonable quiet*—You may not want surroundings so still that a dropping pin will sound like a cannon roar, but a low decibel level will make it easier for you to concentrate.

In some cases, this may require dictating at a time when noisy activities are at a minimum. For example, one manager whose office adjoined a loading bay did his dictation between 2:30 p.m. and 4:30 p.m., hours in which deliveries and shipments were infrequent.

Dictaters may have to make positive moves to ensure quiet. A colleague in a neighboring office, in love with Bach and Beethoven, may have to be asked to lower the volume of the radio during regular working hours.

•*Lighting*—In most cases, the light you have for ordinary writing and working purposes is adequate for dictation. However, you may want to check how satisfactory the lighting is on hand-held material when you sit in your normal dictation position.

Of course, if you are working with a stenographer, lighting in his or her work area must be good enough to avoid any reading or writing problem.

•*Air quality*—Obviously you'd like this to be satisfactory throughout your working day. The only reason for mentioning it here is that, where your dictation requires special concentration, particularly over a period of time, stuffiness, too high or too low temperatures may make it more difficult for you to keep your mind on your work.

•*Your chair*—What's true of air quality applies to your chair. You want to sit in comfort at all times. If, in the course of protracted dictation, you find your chair gives you the fidgets and no adjustment is possible, you may want to consider a replacement.

•*Desk, auxiliary table, etc.*—In the ordinary course of working, people tend to use their desk-tops to hold notes, background materials, and other reference matter to be consulted. However, when a considerable amount of material is used—as in the course of dictating a lengthy report—you may want an additional table or stand within easy reach of where you're sitting.

•*Location of your "listener"*—Whether you work with a stenographer or dictating apparatus, location is an important consideration.

If you use a recorder, you want it in easy reach (on your desk or on a separate stand). Remember, you want to be able to talk in normal tones.

If you're working with a stenographer, his or her convenience and comfort are major considerations. In addition to the conveniences of light, comfortable chair, etc., the stenographer must be close enough to hear your voice easily and clearly.

Materials You Need

The materials on which dictation is based should be minimal. For example, if you're doing several letters, all you may require is a list of your correspondence with a word or two on the subject of each communication. However, as the material to be dictated becomes more extensive or complicated, additions may have to be made.

•*Files, dossiers, etc.*—When your communication involves previous events, you may require the file containing information about them. For example, if you're writing a memo to your personnel director about the performance and attendance record of one of your subordinates, the individual's work file may go back for several years and include everything from the individual's safety record to performance reviews.

•*Reports and records*—Some of your communications and correspondence may deal with studies that have been made or routine records that have been kept. For example, your boss may have asked for a review of your department's production of a particular item during the last quarter. You may need an entire quarter's weekly reports in order to respond satisfactorily.

•*Reference material*—For certain kinds of communication, you may need everything from a foreign-language dictionary to an encyclopedia, or a compendium of members of a trade association.

Keep the materials you need at hand. Dictation should not be interrupted while someone fishes out material for you or you do the hunting. As far as reference material is concerned, it's helpful to use paper markers which flag particular sections. This also cuts down on paper shuffling during dictation.

Developing Your Thoughts

Some people are more verbally spontaneous than others. However, spontaneity is not the only requirement for being able to put words together to form the message you want to send. For brief letters and memos, and those that are routine, a cue word or two can trigger your thinking and help you dictate your communication. A piece of any length or intricacy requires you to pre-think your ideas, and preferably put your thoughts in the form of a logical outline (for more about this point, see Chapter 7, Cues and Outlines—the Helpful Links).

One fact that my dictation workshop (organized as one aspect of the research for this book) made clear is that no two people even using the identical outline, will end up with the same material. Think *about* and *through* your subject, developing what you want to say relevant to the subject or point at issue.

Keep a Sharp Focus

We all have a tendency to digress, to drag in subject matter from left field. Digression, when it is intended, is fine. You may want to go out of your way to make sure a particular point is understood. You may want to depart from your subject temporarily to make a point that only indirectly relates to the business at hand, but is relevant nevertheless.

However, to keep the reader interested, to make it easier for him or her to grasp what is being said, it is necessary that you be clear in your own mind as to exactly what the subject area is. This is true when developing an outline or when actually dictating. Straying into unrelated territory is a waste of time for you and the recipient.

Incorporate Visual and Quoted Material

You can simplify matters and save time when graphics or other visual material is to be part of your message or report. Let the secretary or typist know—by instructions given in advance—that such material is to be included. Your instructions should explain the positioning. Then, attach the material to the cassette, hand it to the secretary, or send it to the WP center with labeling that makes it clear how and where it is to be added to your dictation.

Aim for Perfection?

This point is worth special attention. It seems to be self-contradictory, but isn't.

Obviously, you don't want to make mistakes in your dictation. There is a saving all around if the transcription yields a final, perfect draft. But, even experienced dictaters must feel free to make mistakes because they should get a chance to correct and edit the first draft. Hesitation, even writers' block, would cramp their dictation style if they lacked this freedom. Further, it should be made clear that the opportunity to edit and improve copy is one of the strengths of dictation.

Since a special virtue of WP systems is that errors can be corrected swiftly, and at relatively small cost, you are taking advantage of a WP strong point by not permitting fear of error to constrict you.

Your Daily Energy Cycle

We've already mentioned the value of doing your dictation at a time when noise and interruptions are at a minimum. In addition, individuals vary as to their peak energy level. For example, some people are at their sharpest in the morning. Others tend to start slow and work up to a high point in the afternoon.

Undoubtedly, you've observed it in yourself: Your energies have regular peaks and valleys. There are times during the working day that you feel up to anything; other times you would just as soon coast along.

The well-known industrial psychologist Norman R. F. Maier studied the working efficiency of a group of executives, and charted his findings as illustrated in Figure 4-1. Remember that the curve represents the rise and fall in efficiency of the "average." Your own personal energies may closely resemble those charted, or deviate somewhat. In any event, the same factors apply:

• *Warm-up period*—Note the rise from the morning start. Physiologists explain the warm-up on a partially physical basis. Muscles must be limbered; changes in blood pressure and circulation take place.

• *Fatigue drop*—Fatigue is the usual explanation given for the lowering of efficiency in the course of the working period. In some cases, this tends to be cumulative.

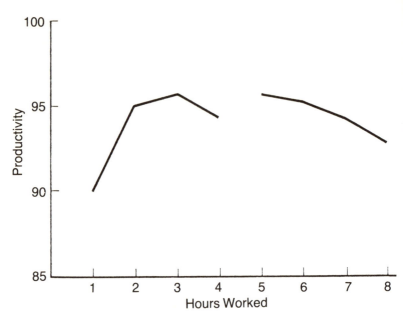

Figure 4-1. This personal efficiency chart was plotted by industrial psychologist Norman R. F. Maier during his study of the working efficiency of several executives. The curve represents the average efficiency of the group.

•*End spurt*—Although not shown on the chart (Figure 4-1), there is a tendency for efficiency to increase as the end of the work period is approached. In some cases, a similar increase may occur before breaks in general—lunch periods, completion of a task, and so on.

To chart your own ups and downs of daily efficiency, keep a brief record, noting:

1. The hours you feel the peppiest.
2. The times fatigue catches up with you.
3. The periods you feel most at ease mentally.
4. The times you find it difficult to work.

Tabulate the results over several days to pinpoint your strong and weak periods. Then, tailor your daily working schedule to your personal chart. For instance, save tough, demanding jobs for high-energy periods. Fit routine tasks into low-energy periods. Fill in mental doldrums with the tasks that almost "do themselves." Tackle new projects, or mentally taxing ones, when your energy peaks are highest.

Your State of Mind

To some people, dictation is just another part of the job, and that's fine. There's no intention here to build a mystique around the procedure.

However, many of us are aware that if we're "up," if we feel relaxed but energetic, we function better. Some pointers on how to optimize your state of mind can make a material difference in how well you dictate. One of the most helpful assists you can give yourself is to pick the time for your dictation carefully.

We've already mentioned the value of doing your dictation at a time when the noise level and interruptions are at a minimum, and when your energy level is optimum, as suggested by the Maier chart (Figure 4-1). There's another factor: People's moods normally fluctuate. The normal workday may have peaks and valleys of emotions ranging from a pleasant, relaxed state to a tense, nervous one.

In the average case, the work goes along almost regardless of your emotions—as long as they stay within "normal" range. However, if negative emotions surface, if you're angry or upset, it's unwise to dictate. The quality of the work is sure to suffer as a consequence.

There are two possible threats from a negative mood. One, as suggested above, is that the quality of your dictation will be poor. But another related consequence is that the nature of the message may be affected. A letter dictated in anger, es-

pecially if the recipient is the object of that emotion, is likely
to convey feelings that may be overly strong and temporary.

If you are angry or upset, hold off until you have quieted
down before dictating your message. But if you don't, and
the scathing, angry, accusatory message has been dictated in
the heat of emotion, make sure the message isn't sent the
same day.

This delay is an established procedure. Most experienced
secretaries will intentionally not return such a letter for signature until the negative mood has faded. This gives the dictater an opportunity to objectively reconsider the message.

What Not to Dictate

Don't tax yourself or the typist by dictating material that
shouldn't be dictated. The kinds of things that should not
be dictated are:

●*Very short messages*—Some of your letters, certainly
some of your memos, are so brief that dictating them would
represent a waste of time. For example: "Meeting O.K. for
two o'clock," or "Thanks for the report, just what I wanted."

Both of these can be written in longhand on memo note-
paper, addressed, and dropped into your outbox faster than
you can go through the dictation process.

Note: One of the dictation workshop participants took
issue with the point above: "I've taken a batch of short
memos, and with the help of a secretary, polished off about
ten of them in a very short time. I'm sure it went faster
than if I had written or typed them myself."

I concede the point on two conditions: First, that you
have a secretary rather than a WP unit. Mobilizing the resour-
ces of a unit for a message that in total consists of, "O.K. at
five o'clock," doesn't seem to be efficient.

And second, that you have a secretary who is familiar with
the formats and recipients of your notes, so that the dictater

doesn't have to supply these. In most cases, the instructions could take longer than the message itself.

•*Chart or other visual material*—A communication that requires a sketch, or layout, with a minimum of typing is not a good candidate for dictation. (The energy-level chart shown in Figure 4-1 is an example.)

However, a cooperative typist might be able to take your sketch or drawing and, working from a duplicate with handwritten headings and captions, type the words, phrases, and so on, on the original.

•*Secret or confidential material*—There is always a possibility that someone unauthorized to do so will read your material in the course of its being processed. Where security is desired, a possible alternative is to have the material typed under secured circumstances—private room, etc.—by some trustworthy and discreet person, either within the organization or outside.

•*Subjects that require discussion*—Some communications are better made face to face. The other person has an opportunity to respond to what you say as you say it. For this type of exchange, the written word becomes an unwieldy obstacle to reaching an understanding.

•*Urgent matters*—The written word is not adequate for situations that are important and breaking rapidly. Use the phone or face-to-face conversation for subjects that have to be dealt with at once.

Part II.
Three Ways to Prepare

5.
Pre-Thinking
Your Writing

A very important part of your writing takes place well before you push the dictate button on your recorder. This is the pre-thinking stage during which you select, organize, and refine your thoughts about the subject.

An often-discussed bit of musical lore illustrates how this process may take place: Legend has it that on the day the opera, "The Magic Flute," was first performed, someone reminded Mozart that there still wasn't any overture. The composer sat down and dashed off the magnificent overture in time to give the score to the orchestra. If this legend is true, the chances are that Mozart must have "precomposed" the overture in his mind days before he put it down on paper. Leaving the actual writing until just before the deadline may not have been as risky as it seemed at the time.

Context for Your Pre-Thinking

The kind of thinking that the Mozart incident illustrates—and which is paralleled by many creative people—doesn't take place in a vacuum. Conditions which will stimulate the subconscious to perform must be created.

If you have a writing project with a distant deadline, and you don't feel like starting the actual writing right away, then don't. But do draw up a rough outline. See how much information you already have available and how much more you will have to dig out. Decide when you should start this digging out so that the information will be available at the proper time. And, if it would help, discuss the outline for the project with your boss or a colleague. That way, you will not only get a feel for the emphasis needed, but you will be giving your subconscious mind a chance to come up with ideas while the project is incubating.

To develop useful ideas, your subconscious should have some sort of framework that may be filled in for you at odd moments—before falling asleep, while waiting your turn with the dentist, and so on. If you wait till the last minute to prepare an outline or think about an approach, all your subconscious can do is provide you with a feeling of anxiety. But, you can sidestep the hazards and gain the benefits by putting your subconscious to work.

Helping Your Subconscious Work for You

Every great idea, from the wheel to Edison's vacuum tube to Einstein's theory of relativity, sprang largely from the subconscious. You may not have to invent the wheel all over again, but your subconscious mind can help you solve problems in your dictation material that need creative answers. For example:

> Elaine Hammer is asked by her boss to come up with a program for the company's summer picnic. It's a big event, and Hammer's boss wants a new and original approach. For several weeks, Elaine Hammer steeps herself in as much of the history of the company's picnics as is possible. She peruses programs of previous years, talks to people who attended them, asks what they liked and disliked, interviews people who served on last year's program committee.

After filling the mental storehouse with ideas, comments, and requests—the source on which the subconscious draws—she comes up with a brainstorm: a theme picnic keyed to the company's 50th anniversary, which the picnic celebrates. While the basic approach is fairly obvious, her preparation has given her many ideas that can make all the difference to an exciting occasion.

Now, in a memo to her boss, Hammer can be specific about her ideas, from an interest-building publicity campaign built around posters with a huge number 50, followed by a series of pieces in the house organ describing the company's founding, complete with photographs. One of the big events of the day will be the awarding of prizes to people with the most interesting, and oldest, item of memorabilia harking back to the company's beginning half a century ago, etc., etc.

How can you control the inspirations, bright ideas, or solutions to problems that almost literally seem to spring to mind? Here are some steps (suggested by research at the PSI Communications Project at the New Jersey Institute of Technology) to stimulate your subconscious mind to operate on problem areas you select.

•*Relax*—Relaxation doesn't always just happen. Sometimes you have to work for it. In a tense situation, the muscles of the neck and shoulders, the mouth, and tongue tend to tighten. These physical tensions reinforce mental strain and restrict thinking.

When you find yourself under pressure to solve a problem involved in your communication with others, stop for a minute and feel where the tension is in your body. Relax these places by first tensing them for ten seconds and then letting go. Knead the muscles of the neck and legs with your fingers. Loosely shake your limbs. Roll your head slowly from side to side.

Your office isn't a gymnasium, but you'll find that a minute or two of relaxation will help you loosen up your mental muscles and allow ideas to flow more freely.

•*Immerse yourself in the problem*—This is what Elaine Hammer did, and the staff of the PSI Communications Project approves. It says that creativity works best when you immerse yourself in a problem, then step back and let the subconscious take over. Your mind should remain calm, and you should not let anything distract you. If that should happen, gently nudge your mind back to the problem at hand.

•*Trust your subconscious*—Some people doubt their subconscious mind when there is no reason to. Remember, there's a risk in any decision, no matter how carefully planned. On the other hand, don't assume that an idea is guaranteed, or a solution failsafe, just because it seems inspired. Before committing your ideas or answers to paper— or to a secretary or recording machine—test them, if possible.

Questions to Ask

Asking basic questions about the subject matter can help the pre-thinking process:

What's It About?

Your precise subject must be clear in your own mind. For example: You want to write to your boss about a maintenance problem in your department. Accordingly, you don't include remarks about the company picnic, or some second thoughts about the production meeting the day before. Usually, it's wise to confine yourself to a single topic instead of making a memo or report a grab-bag of varied content.

In addition, to make the writing job simpler and to heighten impact, professional writers do what they call "sharpening the focus" of a subject. Let's say a supervisor wants to communicate with the head of personnel on absenteeism in the department. If the subject is "absenteeism," the supervisor is out in a vast, limitless ocean of facts and figures. But, if the subject is confined to "Absenteeism in the assembly department," the job is cut down to practical size. Then, if the supervisor wants to further sharpen the focus, the subject becomes "absenteeism in the assembly department for the first six months of the year." The target is even more clear-cut.

What Are the Key Ideas?

The subject generally guides you. And here is where the habit of making notes can help. A key message of this book is that the spoken word is faster than the written one. However, there is one occasion when longhand can be of help. In pre-thinking your dictation, key ideas may come to you. It's desirable to note these. If a pocket recorder isn't available, brief longhand notes can be a starting point from which to develop an idea in full—and put it on tape.

What Shall I Include?

On every subject of human importance, there's an inexhaustible supply of facts. You have to draw a line. If you include too much, you bore your readers, or drown them in information. If there's too little, you'll mystify or confuse them.

Before you can tell what facts are needed, you have to decide what facts are already known by your audience. In this respect, your job is easier than that of a professional writer. Professional writers usually address themselves to a huge, unseen audience. But generally you are writing to one person, or just a handful of people, and you have a fairly definite picture of what they are like in terms of their interests; pressures on them; past connection with the subject matter; and their objectives in relation to the subject.

Just by way of flexing your mental muscles, consider this problem:

> You're the head of a typing pool. You read about a new kind of copy-holder in an office-methods magazine and want the typists to have them. Imagine that you are about to write to Mr. Gray, your immediate superior, asking him to O.K. the necessary expenditure. Now examine each of these items:
>
> 1. His interests: Is he bored by discussion of detailed departmental operations? Does he have any special concern about the particular operation involved in the equipment you're discussing?
> 2. The pressure on him: Compared with the other matters demanding his attention, will this look unimportant to him?
> 3. His past contact: Does he have experience in such matters so that you can afford to omit many details?
> 4. His objectives: What does he want from your department and how do his objectives relate to your proposition? Is he interested in greater volume of work, or is he out to cut costs? Is he concerned about quality performance, or is he looking these days into employee attitudes?

Once you have answered these and similar questions, your thinking is on its way. Now you have a standard against which to choose and reject ideas. You know how much detail to include or what is better omitted.

Why Am I Writing?

Purpose is paramount. Your objective should be made clear by your memo, letter, or proposal. For example: A manager asks himself the question and develops his answer, "I'm writing this report to clarify the hazards we run into if the piping system in the pump room is not given immediate attention."

Who Are the Recipients?

Are you writing to an individual, a small group or "to all employees"? The answer to this question is important. It helps you resolve such matters as:

1. Vocabulary. You might use sophisticated terminology with your boss, and more simple language if you were sending a communication to a group.
2. Relevance. If you write to the front office about an idea for improving productivity in your department, you may very well talk about costs in some detail. Taking up the same subject with a group of subordinates may cause you to omit cost considerations altogether and dwell on the results you are hoping to achieve.
3. Tone. If you're writing to a colleague, you probably will use a friendly, informal approach. If you're addressing one of the top people in your organization, you would probably choose a more formal approach.

Part II.
Three Ways to Prepare

6.
Psyching Yourself Up

The more positive your attitude—the more you feel in command—the better your dictation is likely to be. But if you are among those with doubts, "psyching up" to heighten your emotional preparedness is particularly appropriate because dictation has a large psychological component. Everything from your personality to your state of mind are factors in your effectiveness. This chapter examines some psychological considerations that can be keys to higher-level achievement.

Seven Steps to Self-Confidence

Psychological hurdles may interfere with your feelings of control and confidence. These obstacles may be put in the form of questions, the answers to which can smooth your way.

Can I Dictate with Complete Mastery?

Some people ask this question when they are beginners. Others ask the same question out of disappointment and frustration after having dictated for some time.

•*Everyone who can talk can dictate*—I talked to one manager about being patched into a word-processing system for the first time. The manager registered real doubt and some fear about being able to dictate. Within just a few minutes, I was able to encourage the manager to dictate some current correspondence. Much to the manager's surprise, it was easy.

Even though dictation isn't "the same" as talking, the ability to verbalize is a fundamental ingredient. I had just suggested that she tell me what the memo she wanted to send would say. Once she got to talking, she was dictating.

•*Excellence is a matter of practicing the right way*—Experience certainly helps. But experience in ineffective or partial methods will mean only limited control. To master the skill and thereby win the ultimate benefits requires a systematic approach that gives you a command of your material and of the finished product. The total approach described here, and especially the review material contained in Chapter 11, Sharpening Your Skills, can provide the boost required for a satisfactory level of mastery.

Secretary vs. Machine, Which Is Better?

For the forseeable future, people will be dictating to both stenographers and dictating machines. The trend is clear—the use of word processing systems is proliferating, and by comparison, the relative number of professional stenographers is declining. Nevertheless, the question, Which is better, secretary or dictating machine?, is unanswerable. Neither is better, Each has advantages and disadvantages.

Advantages of having a secretary include:

1. Useful rapport can exist between steno and dictater.
2. Can make corrections on the spot, and supply quick readbacks.

3. Can be helpful in giving instant feedback to dictater (in terms of reaction to wording, ideas, etc.) Can ask questions immediately if something is not clear.

Disadvantages include:

1. Usually works eight-hour day or less, and may resist overtime.
2. May tire after an hour or so.
3. If steno is absent from work and has not completed transcription of notes, chances are no substitutes can read the shorthand. This means a delay until steno returns to work.
4. A good secretary may be hard to find.

Advantages of a dictating machine:

1. Doesn't complain, has no personal habits or traits that can irritate you. For example, doesn't chew gum, or get long calls from friends or family.
2. Available twenty-four hours a day, and is tireless.
3. Some people are less self-conscious when they dictate to a machine. There is no need to apologize for pauses or interruptions.
4. Conserves secretarial time, and can easily be taken along on a business trip.

Disadvantages include:

1. Can lend themselves to corrections, but some people find machines difficult in this respect.
2. Cannot supply a missing word or phrase.
3. If transcriber has difficulty in discerning some words or phrases dictated, the dictater may not always be available to be asked.
4. Transcriber might feel it's a waste of time to listen to the entire recording before typing it, preferring to take it

down in shorthand to facilitate transcription of corrections, changes, and punctuation.

What About Voice Quality?

It's a common experience: "The first time I heard my
voice played back on a tape recorder," an office manager told
me, "I was shocked. I couldn't believe that hesitant, squeaky
voice was mine . . ."

People new to dictation tend to be self-conscious about
their voice quality, particularly if they have played back a
recording and are disappointed in what they hear. However,
this is usually a temporary concern. What happens is that
with practice the dictater becomes less self-conscious, and
that strained, high-pitched voice turns mellow. The more a
person dictates, the surer and more professional the person
sounds.

How Do I Relate to a Machine?

The first advantage of working with a stenographer, mentioned earlier, suggests that there can be an advantage because
of the "team" factor that is created. Does it follow, then,
that working with a machine is a sterile relationship? Not
necessarily. People who use dictating equipment effectively
tell me that it can be as "human" an experience as dictating to a secretary. What makes this possible is that the dictater does not talk to the machine, but to the target people
dictationese is addressed to. They are, in turn, the transcriber
and the person to whom the message is addressed.

How Do I Build Rapport with a Stenographer?

A good working relationship can be a major help in improving the effectiveness of a dictater-secretary team. Certainly for the dictater who is about to start working with a

new stenographer, or to an experienced person who wants to review this key relationship, rapport is essential. Some guidelines for building rapport:

•*Strive for a friendly quality*—It's not that you want to let barriers down, but dictation will flow more easily in an informal climate.

•*Give some thought to the other's comfort*—Presumably, for your own effectiveness, you will want to make sure your physical situation is satisfactory (comfortable chair, adequate lighting, and so on). Give the stenographer the benefit of the same kind of consideration. It will certainly be greatly appreciated.

•*Suit your pace to the stenographer's*—There will be difficulties if you dictate at a faster or slower rate than the stenographer can record. The signs are clear—signs of discomfort and confusion generally mean you're going too fast and some of your words are either getting lost or garbled.

•*Fidgeting*—A secretary who stares off into space, or taps an impatient pencil on the edge of the dictation pad is registering boredom at the slowness of the dictation. If this happens often, a dictater will have to either figure out how to increase speed (perhaps by better preparation) or try to get a stenographer whose cruising stenographic rate is a better match for the dictation.

How Do I Minimize Tension?

Some people may not even understand the question. "Why," they might say, "should I feel tense when I dictate?" But the fact is, some people do. One of the workshop participants said, for example, "To me, dictating is like making a speech. And I become tense for that reason." Other people who are new to machine dictating might start with a certain amount of apprehension that can best be described by the phrase, "mike fright." The parallel situation, working with a secretary, might lead to self-consciousness.

For some people, the solution is to accept the tension as a matter of course, and go on with the business of dictating. For others, there is reassurance in the thought that this type of tension is usually the result of inexperience. The more one dictates the less likely it is that tension will be a problem.

How Do I Optimize My Mood?

This question was asked by a woman who has been dictating for some years and realizes that any negative mood represents an obstacle to effective dictation. While it's true that emotional upset can interfere, you can't always be tranquil, certainly not under the pressure of the business scene. Here are some suggestions:

1. If the upset is severe enough, postpone the dictation.
2. If negative emotion is something you feel you can minimize, take a break, go for a walk, or have a cup of coffee until the upset subsides.
3. Concentrate on the content of your message. If it's important enough to dictate, it deserves your involvement.

You Are Not Alone

A basic feeling of insecurity afflicts some word originators. It's a feeling that may very well diminish once the dictater remembers that a number of capable people are available for assistance. Secretaries have been helping their bosses ever since the first secretary entered the world of business. As a matter of fact, management expert Peter Drucker says, half in jest, "An executive is only as good as his secretary helps him or her to be."

And, as for the competence of word-processing personnel, by and large the level of intelligence and capability of these people is superior. Remember, too, that technology in the field is advancing at a great rate. Last year's "latest" in equipment may already be obsolete by newer, better, more flexible pieces of equipment, capable of making your life as a dictater even easier.

In short, the dictater can usually get the help that's needed. Essentially, it's a matter of teamwork, and you're in the position to be captain of the team.

7.
Cues and Outlines—
the Helpful Links

One of the most helpful preparatory steps you can take is to put down on paper material that provides a springboard into your dictation. This material can be of two kinds: cues and outlines. These two elements stimulate your thinking and form a bridge between thought and verbalizing.

Cues

Cues are words, phrases, or sentences that suggest what you want to say. Unlike an outline, which is a kind of framework, cues are like triggers, often personalized and meaningful only to you. Some examples:

•*Working with a wonderful team*—A marketing vice president put that cue on a note from his secretary that the twentieth anniversary with the company was at hand for one of their top salesmen. Using that cue later on, he dictated:

Dear Gordon and Kay:

What a privilege it's been to know you both during these years!

When one can work with someone like you, Gordon—intelligent, creative, loyal and always kind and thoughtful. . . And always with beautiful Kay, who has been as interested in your career and our organization as any man or woman could be. . . then that's something!

May all the years to come be rewarding and fun. May we always be friends. Susan joins me in congratulations and best wishes.

> Sincerely,
> Joe

●*Thanks-but-no-thanks*—This note on a letter of invitation to a conference that the sender didn't want to attend was sufficient for a two-paragraph letter:

Dear Paul:

Many thanks for inviting me to your association dinner. As you remember, I attended last year and enjoyed the proceedings hugely. At the time, I was particularly impressed by the fine job your committee had done in preparing an outstanding program.

Unfortunately, much as I would like to be with you this year, a prior commitment will find me in St. Paul on the evening of your dinner. I hope I'll be luckier next year. And thanks again.

> Sincerely,
> Brad

How and When to Use Cues

Here are the factors that favor using cues:

●*A brief message*—Cues are fine for letters, memos and other short messages. Longer messages, or complicated ones, usually require an outline.

●*You have the kind of mind that responds to key words and ideas*—Some people use cues easily. The appropriate thoughts and words flow readily when the trigger is pulled. If you are in this group, cues are for you.

•*You have the knack of expressing the theme or heart of a message succinctly*—Your cue word or phrase doesn't have to be witty or literary, and should be brief and to the point. It needn't be understandable to anyone else. If it works for you, it's the perfect cue.

The simplest place for a cue, if it's a reply, is on the communication you received. Then you have the message to which you are responding and your cue for the answer on a single sheet of paper.

If you're originating the exchange, and particularly if you have several such communications, you can note the cues as one personnel director did, first listing the recipient or addressee, then his cue:

> Memo to all employees: "Get ready for the company picnic"
> To Grace Fayne, head of R & D: "Still trying to find you a physicist"
> To Sam Webster: "Happy birthday"
> To Jack T, asking if his wife can apply for a job in his department: "Sorry, against policy"
> To benefits administrator, setting up a meeting: "Expanded program"

Outlines

Outlines are a framework for your writing. They are most useful when:

1. The piece you want to write is lengthy.
2. The material is complicated, therefore a logical presentation is necessary for the reader to understand.
3. When you want to divide the material in such a way that it will help all readers grasp your central ideas readily, and also will assist in partial reading. For example: Manager Grace Heflin is presenting a report to a management group on quality control results. The outline is carried into the finished text in the form of headings, and clearly identifies each phase—personnel; procedure;

new methods; and this quarter's results compared to last. Some people getting this report will skim the first part quickly and go to what, for them, is the heart of the matter, the improvement or lack of it in inspection results for the present quarterly operating period. These results are in a subsection of the outline. The presentation will clearly indicate the start of the subsection with a main head, "This Quarter's Results Compared to Last."

What Kind of Outline to Use

There is a difference of opinion about outlines. Some people say, "I couldn't dictate a page of copy without some kind of framework." Others insist that they "can't work with an outline." And some add to this statement, "An outline interferes with my thinking."

Obviously, people should be permitted to write in any way they please. Writing is a creative process and, in many aspects, creativity is not logical but psychological.

In years of working as a professional writer, associated with staffs of writers with a broad range of experience and skill, it is my considered opinion that the people who work without outlines, trying to ad lib a whole report or any long piece of writing, usually are those who have trouble organizing and dictating the material.

Perhaps one of the reasons some people shy away from outlines is that there's some confusion as to just what an outline is. Certainly there are several possibilities. And since it is likely that people who have difficulty with outlines are really saying they have never found a method of outlining that works for them, the following may be of particular help to these as well as of assistance to word originators at large.

There are three approaches (the *cue outline, general outline*, and the *specific outline*) that can help you structure your material, put it in order in such a way that it will be easier to dictate, and easier for a reader to understand your finished product.

The Cue Outline

We previously talked about cues as an aid for writing short pieces (memos, letters, and so on). These word or phrase triggers can also be used to help you do pieces of medium length (from one to six pages). This type of outline consists of a number of cues placed in some kind of logical order. Here's how a department head used a series of cues to help him with a rundown of the attendance situation among the personnel in his department for submission to his boss. His cue words were:

1. *Arithmetic*—By this he meant the absenteeism figures (number of people on the roster, number absent, the various attendance rates in terms of percentages).
2. *Why?*—Reasons given for absence. Here the report reflected interviews that the department head had with each absentee on his or her return to work.
3. *Problem cases*—He wanted to stress the relatively small number of people who were contributing the major boost to the absentee figures.
4. *Pete, Harry and Phyllis*—This was the department head's reminder to mention three exceptional cases where health matters and family relationships represented special difficulties.
5. *Moves?*—This cue was to state a number of possible actions he might take to deal with the problem.
6. *Recommendation*—He wanted his report to be positive, to suggest a course of action concentrating on the few individuals who were the major cause of his department's poor attendance record.
7. *Meet with*—In his conclusion, he asked his boss to set a

convenient time for a get-together at which specific remedies would be agreed upon.

The cue sequence differs from other approaches to outlining in one respect: the cue words or phrases are *suggestive*. For instance, they are not like general outlines, in which a sequence of words or phrases are standard and may be used for a wide range of subject matter. The cue sequence consists of triggers that have special meaning for the word originator, and reflects the specific content of the material to be written.

When to Use the Cue Outline

The sequence-of-cues method can be useful when you are completely familiar with your material, or when there is no major problem with organizing the material. This could be the case when what you have to say is fairly straightforward, and may have a ready-made chronology. For example: A credit manager wanted to call the treasurer's attention to the situation with a big account. His cues followed a natural time sequence: *Things O.K. in January; Two months later; End of the half-year period*; and *Present status, blah.*

Some subjects have a built-in logical sequence. The head of an inspection department wrote a report on a special job titled "Quality Control Results of Prentiss Job # 789". His cues: *Specs and T's* (tolerances); *How we measured; Results we got; Breakdown of Rejects*; and *How to do job next time.*

The sequence-of-cues method can also be used when reference material is at hand. One originator is particularly skillful at using a cue that refers him to a particular news clipping, magazine article, or other printed source. His cue might read, *"Wall Street Journal story, page 1."* Then, skimming the red-circled paragraphs he has marked out, he either quotes or paraphrases the relevant passage.

The General Outline

There are several generalized structures for written material that are simple and useful. For example, junior executive

Mary Heller wants to let her boss know how she's been performing in her job for the last six months. (You won't be too far wrong if you assume she has a raise on her mind.) She makes up an outline that looks like the following:

Introduction

Opening statement: "The growth of activity in my department, along with the increased responsibility I've been taking on, suggests that a review of my performance is in order."

Supporting material. Here, the executive brings to bear the developments in her job in the last six months that support her request for a salary increase.

Conclusion: "I hope we can get together to discuss this matter at the end of the week, after you've had an opportunity to investigate the facts. . ."

Other general outlines that can help you develop a simple framework for your material should include the *Opening*, the *Development*, and the *Conclusion*. One used by managers in presenting a solution to a problem they feel they have licked includes *Identification of problem, Analysis*, and *Recommendations*.

General outlines are best used when:

1. The material you want to write is long but uncomplicated.
2. When you want to rough out an outline for a subject, in part to help you think it through.
3. The material falls naturally into a sequence of major sections. For example, an executive wants to tell her boss about an experimental project. The simple way to present the material is under the headings, *past, present,* and *future*.

Specific Outlines

Specific outlines reflect the subject matter directly. The words and phrases making up the outline should not be general, but rather specific to the subject you want to write about. This type of outline is the most used, and the most useful in helping you pre-think material for longer pieces.

How to Develop a Specific Outline

Here is the approach by which you can develop such an outline. Let's say you are an office manager who wants to send a proposal to the boss for revamping the filing area in your department. After giving the problem some thought, you are ready to make up an outline. To some extent, you're counting on the outline to help you round out your coverage of the subject. You reach for a sheet of paper and a pencil, and begin to make notes, to list ideas, putting them down in the form of words or phrases. Here is a list of ideas relating to the filing-area move as they might come to mind:

1. Relieve bottleneck
2. Overtime averages 30 hours per month
3. Employees griping about last-minute notice of over-time
4. Will cut costs
5. Better filing needed
6. Will cut down on misfiles
7. Will talk it over with superior
8. Suited to our operation
9. Absenteeism also caused work
10. Got ideas from management case history
11. Last year's troubles
12. Minimize errors
13. Will provide more aisle space
14. Expenditure would pay for itself quickly
15. Better service to other departments
16. Easier to teach to new employees
17. Send "old" file cabinets to storage

Some people feel their thinking is crisper if they put each idea in the form of a complete sentence. There is no universal best way. Whether you choose to use whole sentences or phrases depends on your own mental make-up. Experiment with each, see which suits you better.

How can you be sure you have listed all the relevant items? Here again, it pays to borrow from the professional. The journalist has a set of questions to make sure that nothing important has been ignored:

1. *Who?* (Get clear on the people involved in the situation you are discussing. Who is affected—your boss, other executives, fellow supervisors, employees, customers, suppliers? Who caused it? Who should be consulted? Who can add information?)
2. *What?* (Here you consider the specific facts of what happened or will happen—conditions, circumstances, events. For example: "The department has been handling three times as much work as last year; we have not added more employees and do not intend to; we hope the proposed change will help . . .")
3. *Why?* (Here you deal with explanations. The key word is *because*: "The change is needed because . . ." The answer will show the relationship between things, spelling out cause and effect.)
4. *Where?* (It may be important to discuss where the situation is happening or will happen. For example, a proposal for a change might be rejected if the reader thought the idea applied to areas outside the jurisdiction of the person making the proposal.)
5. *When?* (This question, unanswered, also can land your memo or report in the basket. Failure to refer to the time element might lead to those sad post-mortems that begin with: "But I thought you meant it had already been done," or, "Why didn't you say we had to decide before the end of the month?"
6. *Which?* (They point out that in most situations there are alternatives. "It should always be made clear

which of two or more things already mentioned is being discussed." That's a good rule in thinking about your material and in actually writing it.)

7. *How much?* (There should never be any doubt left as to how much or how long. To talk quantities ensures your being specific.)

8. *How many?* (There should never be any doubt left as to how many.)

Ask yourself these questions, and, from the answers, select those you want to include.

How to Fit the Facts Together

Every fact in a report or memorandum may be crystal clear; the details may be one hundred percent correct, but readers may throw up their hands at the end and ask: "What's this all about?" They will unless the details are relevant and are arranged in a logical, easy-to-understand, easy-to-follow sequence.

That is the purpose of the outline you are devising. To repeat, an outline serves a double purpose: to help you think through to the relevant aspects of your subject; and, to guide your dictation in the way it should go to cover your subject satisfactorily.

These are two good reasons for outlining your communication. The difference is between going for a rambling walk in the woods and taking a trip by railway. In the first case, you can easily get lost. On the train trip, you're always moving on track toward your destination, and you can always find out where you are.

You continue to prepare your outline by systematically examining the points listed in your notes. Then:

1. Read your notes to get a general impression of how they add up. In doing so, you'll notice that some of them are important, some trivial. Some require lengthy explana-

tion; some need only a sentence or a phrase. For example, in the list of ideas, "last year's troubles" may require three paragraphs, while "got ideas from management case history" may be just a phrase in a sentence: "I think I can solve this problem by adapting an idea I got from . . ."

2. Ask yourself what theme, or single thread, binds together all the items in your notes. You should be able to express that all-inclusive idea in one general sentence. The value of a brief statement telling your whole story is that it gives you, as well as the reader, a guide. You can match up each point against two tests:

●Should the point be included? Is it germane to your central theme? In our example, the item "absenteeism also caused work problems " may be related to the subject of overall efficiency, but it is not relevant to a discussion of a new filing method. You should cross it off your list. Similarly, you find that "will cut down on misfiles" repeats "minimize errors." You could then eliminate one or the other.

●Is the point central to your subject, or only remotely connected? This helps you decide where it belongs in your outline and how much space it should get in your writing.

3. Rearrange the individual items, putting together those that logically relate to each other. This may sound difficult if you've never tried it before. What you do is look for a common heading for each group of ideas that belong together. Of course, different people will see different headings, and will word them differently. In any case, you now arrange the individual items under the headings that seem logical to you.

The rule is: One thought at a time. But in what sequence? Under one heading you may have, say, four ideas. Which should come first? One basic consideration must be kept in mind: Arrange the individual points in the order which your reader will find easiest to understand. Ask yourself: "If I didn't know what this was about, what would I have to know first? Then what? Then what next?"

Sample of a Specific Outline

Here, finally, is the way the outline of a proposal to relocate the equipment in the filing area might look.

I.   *Proposal to Improve Filing Area Layout*
     Send "old file" cabinets to storage
     Got idea from a management case history
II. *The Conditions It Would Correct*
     Better filing needed
     Relieve bottleneck
     Overtime 30 hours per month
     Employees griping about last-minute notice of overtime
     Will cut down on misfiles
     Last year's troubles
     Will provide more aisle space
III. *Feasibility of the Proposal*
     Suited to our operation
     Expenditure would pay for itself
     Better service to other departments
     Easier to teach to new employees
IV. *The Next Steps to Be Taken*
     Would like to talk it over with superior

Introduction and Conclusion of an Outline

You have outlined the body of your communication. But one more step remains—you need an introduction at the beginning, and a conclusion at the end.

Just as the chairman of a meeting cannot introduce a speaker without knowing who he is and what he is going to talk about, you cannot choose an introduction without knowing your content. So don't plan your introduction until you've outlined the body.

For your introduction, pick out what you believe will be most effective in seizing and holding the interest of the person you are addressing. In our sample case, the most likely attention-getter is "will cut costs." Of course, this is in addition to a title, or statement of purpose, that immediately tells what the report is about.

And what about a conclusion? There are several possibilities. In lengthy reports, the most frequently used conclusion—because it's very effective—is to summarize the main points. For example:

> "I hope you will agree that my proposal to change our filing method will correct some current problems. In my judgment, it will surely cut operating costs. If you are interested, let me know when we can get together to talk it over."

It is generally desirable to have an action ending in this type of communication: "I suggest an immediate test of the idea," or, "We could check this new material by placing a sample order. I'll be glad to do this if you give me the go-ahead."

Developing Outline Material

During the dictation workshop, participants having trouble developing an outline for a given subject asked, "How do I get the additional ideas for making up my outline?"

The problem here is one of writing. It is similar to the situation where a novelist turns out a first chapter and then creativity sags, making it difficult to start on chapter two.

One method for developing material has already been suggested—the journalistic approach of answering the questions who, what, why, where, when, which, how much and how many. Another method, which I have developed and taught others to use successfully, makes it possible to develop a subject area, starting from an opening or introductory point. For example:

> A friend of mine, a production executive in a metal fabricating plant, was asked by an editor of a trade journal to do an article on his hobby, wood carving.
>
> My friend, a heck of a good production manager, and an excellent wood carver, was fazed by the writing problem. "After I've said I like to work with wood, what do I say?" he asked me.
>
> "You've got a fine story to tell," I said. "Let's get together and make up an outline."

I didn't intend to talk about the outline, however. I just handed him a sheet of paper on which were typed some key headings that might suggest possible ways to help him come up with new ideas. It was an approach I used myself when I got stuck in developing material.

Subjects can be developed by description, feeling, association analysis, additional detail, opposites, agreement and/ or contradiction:

●*By description*—"I first became interested in wood carving . . ."

●*By feeling*—"It opened a whole new world . . ."

●*By association*—"My carving made me more aware of things about me, furniture, for example . . ."

●*By analysis*—"Why did I like wood carving, and why didn't clay modeling or stone carving turn me on? My years out west in redwood country . . ."

●*By additional detail*—"Learning to use each type of tool was a special adventure. And also, the care of the gouges and chisels, especially honing the edges . . ."

•*By opposites*—"Wood carving is very different from that other creative activity with which I am also familiar, running a production line . . ."

•*By agreement*—"It's taken me some time, but I now agree with those who say that an avocation is a great balancing force for a vocation, and opens up new vistas . . ."

•*By contradiction*—"There are some people who think of a hobby as a kind of thumb-in-mouth preoccupation. They couldn't be more wrong . . ."

My friend felt that with the ideas stimulated by the list, he could now outline the article. The list constitutes a tool that can help people become more aware of the possibilities of a subject. Not all the phrases will produce ideas. Basically, the list pushes you in the direction of free-associating ideas related to your theme or subject. It won't work for everyone, but try it at the next opportunity, and see if it works for you.

Part III.
Four Key Steps

8.
Getting Started

"My problem with dictation," the workshop participant told me, "is getting started."

It's a common ailment but like many simple afflictions the cure is not necessarily simple. Even with a good outline, some people find it difficult to break through the invisible barrier that blocks action.

One interesting aspect of "starting" trouble: It may crop up in connection with a short letter as well as a long report. And, similarly, if you can break through and make a start, you can get rid of a block to a major report as readily as to a short piece.

Developing an Opener

One technique that solves the problem of getting started is to work up an opening sentence or paragraph. It may set a tone, or pin down a thought that propels you into the balance of the piece. For example, here are openers that helped some word originators get going:

> I just read Mr. Bradley's announcement of your resignation, and I have an immediate sense of loss. I remember the great things you did . . .

> Possibly it is a minority opinion, but I am definitely not in favor of a staff meeting off company premises. Let me tell you why . . .

> This report is the work of six people who have given without stint of their energies and intelligence. Here is the record . . .

There are some people for whom even a good opening is not enough to get them rolling. And since the cause of the "freezing up" can be somewhat complex, it pays to dig more deeply into the start-up problem: There are two major reasons that stand in the way of dictation progress—*procrastination* and *writer's block*. Since they represent two basically different problems, they require different treatments.

Procrastination

Of course, the problem of procrastination isn't limited to dictation. Tasks of every kind are put off once, twice, or a dozen times.

Procrastination can prevent a completion of even a simple task. "I could have finished the job in ten minutes," complains a department head, "but somehow I keep delaying." Some possible causes:

•*Fatigue*—In some cases, it's simply a matter of physical or mental tiredness that explains the delay. The obvious solution here is to select a time when you feel physically and emotionally "up." Some people successfully cope with the situation by getting the task taken care of "first thing in the morning," or "right after lunch" when energy levels are likely to be high.

•*Lack of deadline pressure*—"I've had all the time in the world to send that memo to Personnel," an executive says. "But somehow I couldn't get started. . ."

The answer may very well be that having all the time in the world means that there is no incentive to get the job done. One of the virtues of deadlines is that they force you to complete a task by a given time. In some cases, if there is no built-in time requirement, dictaters have been able to create an artificial one: "I'll complete that report by five o'clock on Friday," says a division manager, making a promise to himself he knows he will keep—because he has *said* he would.

•*Concentration difficulties*—An individual may tend to put off a writing assignment because "I just can't put my mind to it." Concentration may be disrupted or interfered with because of worry or preoccupation with other matters. Obviously, the solution is to take care of the distractions, to free yourself to take on the delayed tasks. If this is not feasible—you may be concerned with a problem that is not easily resolved—it may be necessary to take on the task with a lower level of concentration than you would like. If the task is especially demanding in terms of the thought it requires, you may be able to do an adequate job despite your preoccupation by an act of will, forcing yourself to start the dictation.

In general, procrastination is limited to dictation of low or questionable priority. Somehow, everything that must get done gets done. It's the writing task that you are pretty sure no one is waiting for, that is without a sense of urgency, that is usually put off. But needlessly delaying correspondence or other written material often has a destructive effect on the procrastinator. A vague sense of guilt, of not doing one's job, can be a minor but persistent drag. For the sake of your own feeling of effectiveness, as well as the instances when procrastination can delay a necessary task, it is desirable to face up to dilatoriness.

One executive I know says, "I find that the best cure for my own occasional procrastination is to confront it. Once I'm aware that I'm stalling, I just say, 'Cut it out.' And that does it for me."

Eliminating Writer's Block

"Writer's block" is a traditional phrase describing an obstacle from which even professional writers suffer. In the context of this book, perhaps the problem should be called dictater's block, but there's no need to avoid the traditional phrase since dictation is merely a special technique for getting words on paper.

But whatever you call it, writer's block or dictater's, it is frustrating and worrisome not to be able to get going on a writing project. Understanding the causes can be of considerable help in alleviating the problem:

•*Doubt of ability*—"I froze up solid," an office manager told me, "when my boss asked me to do a comprehensive description of the work done in my unit. It was a perfectly reasonable request and I was given enough time. But when days passed and I still found myself unable to start, I decided to try to figure out why. Eventually, I came to understand. I wasn't sure I was going to be able to do the analysis. But once I realized that, it seemed clear that my concern was off base. I was thoroughly familiar with the operations, I had helped develop most of them myself. Once I realized my worry was groundless, I was able to get started. . ."

•*Concern about a detail*—It sometimes happens that a minor problem may stop an entire project cold. I know of an instance when a department head could not bring himself to start an important letter because he wasn't sure what kind of stationery he wanted to use. In another instance, it was uncertainty about the particular phrasing to go into a letter that interfered.

Once you can pinpoint this type of barrier to action, it's generally easy to eliminate it. For example, The department head realized that the particular kind of stationery really was of little importance to the communication. An individual who had fears about choice of words realized that even if the letter didn't turn out to be a literary masterpiece, the thought would be clearly communicated.

•*Fear of commitment*—A manager was asked by his boss to recommend one of three possible procedures for processing orders in his department. Every time he sat down to his dictating machine, he invariably found himself unable to start. Eventually, he realized that the problem was deciding which of the three procedures he should favor. In short, his writer's block was caused by difficulties in making a decision and committing himself to the consequences of it.

When you're asked to state a viewpoint or make a decision, sometimes inability to write about it stems from a reluctance to be identified with a viewpoint that you're not sure about. Clear up the hesitation and you clear up the writer's block at the same time.

•*Insufficient preparation*—A member of the dictation workshop described his blockage problem: "When the dead-, line for an important memo to my boss loomed and I wasn't able to get going, I stopped trying to write and started to figure out why I had the problem. Eventually, I realized that despite the fact that this was an important communication, I had not adequately prepared for dictating it. I wasn't pleased with my outline, and furthermore, it became clear that my supporting material and references were skimpy. Once I took care of these lacks, I was able to proceed."

•*The ego factor*—For many writers, this is the heart of the blockage problem. Whenever you write memos, letters, or reports, you're literally writing *for the record*. This means that you are identified, characterized by the words you put on paper. And once that is done, you are open to the judgment of others. Everyone who faces a judgment is aware that it may be negative.

Understandably, people will avoid sticking their heads through a hole in canvas if they feel that one or more critics are waiting to throw beanbags at them. When fear of criticism is the cause of writer's block, you have to face the fact that you assume a risk when taking a stand. To overcome this difficulty, you must face up to the risk, and become willing to take your chances.

Two Sources of Encouragement

Notice that many of the reasons for writer's block involve a lack of self-confidence. Temporarily you have lost faith in your ability to argue, persuade, or even clearly state your point of view.

Some people find that a simple way to renew their self-confidence is to read their own previously written material: "I just couldn't bring myself to get started on a quarterly report, even though I had done several before. I dug back into my files and began reading the one I had written the previous quarter. It was good stuff! The boost I got from that reading quickly got me started . . ."

Another source of encouragement: Let the second-guessing called editing (see Chapter 10) reassure you. One of the strengths of dictation is that originators can almost always look over the transcript. Anything that is not acceptable may be revised, from typographical errors and your original choice of words, to the tone of what you have written. Remembering that you will have the opportunity to correct and improve your first draft permits you a wide latitude. The head of a Massachusetts engineering firm says, "Some of the letters I send out are in the nature of preliminary contracts. When I dictate those, I don't waste time agonizing over every word. I think of my dictation as a rough draft. Then, with my ideas down in black and white, I can make the changes my final thinking suggests."

Six Ways to Get Started

It isn't necessary to analyze your inner feelings to overcome a reluctance to get going. Some solutions are effective not because they resolve the problem, but because they bypass it. The following suggestions may work for you, at least once. Some can become a permanent solution. The first suggestion certainly could become a habit.

1. Plunge Right In

A colleague of mine says:

> I used to find it . . . difficult to . . . start working. I finally got fed up with myself and just sat down and began making notes for a survey. Then I took right off, began to dictate. Now when I find myself stalling, I just get tough with myself and begin.

2. Reward Yourself

B. F. Skinner would approve of this technique. His major contribution to motivation theory is the concept of positive and negative reinforcement. According to Skinner, people will undertake and repeat behavior that is rewarded. One department head uses the idea this way:

> She hated to dictate the three reports due at the end of the week. Each Friday she went through the same unpleasant ordeal, watching the clock and finally tackling the task at the last possible moment.
>
> Finally, as she says, "I got plain sick of myself." One Friday she made a bet with herself: she would go out to lunch at Jennie's, a good restaurant she frequented only on special occasions, if she finished the reports by noon instead of the usual 4 o'clock deadline. It worked, and she enjoyed her reward. She added, "Eventually starting that job in the morning instead of buckling down at the last moment became a habit. I found that even if I didn't reward myself, I continued to start the dictation early."

3. Play a Game

A supervisor in a utility company says:

> About six months ago my company set up a typing pool, and the secretary I shared with two other people was made office manager. I was given a dictating machine, and although we all had several hours of instruction and practice, I seemed to have more trouble than the others in using the equipment. Whatever the reason, I held off doing my dictation as long as I could, and at times the work piled up pretty high. My boss bawled me out for not taking care of some special correspondence, and I decided I'd better get with it. My schedule is flexible, so I hit on the idea of starting my dictation right after the first office mail delivery in the morning. I stuck to the agreement I had made with myself, and it's been working ever since.

You can pick your own starting gun. Instead of the first mail delivery it might be after the first phone call. You can even make up a different game—as long as it is one you will play.

4. Commit Yourself

"My regular dictation doesn't bother me," a manager says. "It's the big jobs—in my case progress reports—that I block on." He found that he could get himself to undertake these by telling his boss or colleagues, "I'm going to start the report on (some reasonable date)." That way, he locked himself in. He felt committed to start at the time he said he would.

5. Schedule the Start

A supervisor with a heavy work schedule told me:

> My job breaks down into a lot of small pieces, some routine, some of the fire-fighting variety. I plan my work the day before— Tuesday's work Monday evening, and so on. Somehow my corres-

pondence kept getting lost in the shuffle, and at the end of the week, I'd have a full in-box and very little going out. And some of the memos were urgent. I finally realized that I was doing a lousy job of communicating, and ever since, I schedule my dictation. Not necessarily at a definite time, because in my work I have to stay flexible, but I make sure to put it on my "to do" list and fit it in at a reasonable priority.

6. Arrange for Your Dictation

This suggestion somewhat overlaps the previous one, but it differs in that it involves a second person. It is particularly applicable to those who work with a secretary.

"I started getting complaints from people that I wasn't answering their memos, that reports were coming in late and so on," a department head in a New Jersey pharmaceutical firm says. "I share a secretary with another manager. I worked out an arrangement among the three of us that I would do my dictation at a specific time every day. It turned out very well. Not only did the secretary's presence force me to take care of my paperwork, but it helped the secretary and the other manager to schedule their time better."

Part III.
Four Key Steps

9.
Moving Right Along

Once you get started, it's advisable to take advantage of the momentum you're building. Keeping up a satisfactory pace as you dictate is one of the secrets of time-saving.

To some extent, dictation is like a fast motor car. It's capable of high speeds, but it's up to the driver to take advantage of the vehicle's cruising range. There are a number of things you can do that help set a good workpace—that is, one you feel comfortable with, and one at which your thinking and verbalizing work together effectively.

1. Know Your Optimum Workpace

Dictation rate varies from person to person. Also, your own pace can vary, depending on the nature of the material you are working with. Monitor yourself as you dictate. Get a feeling of your "normal" rate, one in which you feel comfortable, in command.

2. Check Workpace Factors

As you dictate, check your pace from time to time to see whether it "feels" right. A number of things influence dictation rate. Your purpose in making a check is to determine whether you're in the groove, progressing at a desirable rate (good speed at which control is at a maximum).

•*Are you forcing?*—Unless you're facing a tough deadline, try not to push yourself past what you consider a normal rate. You may lose more in the quality of your dictation than you gain in quantity.

•*Are you lagging?*—Poor concentration, distractions, or worry about personal matters can slow you down. Try to eliminate any such obstacles. It may even pay—in the case of serious concern about some personal matter—to put off the dictation for a while in the hope that your ability to concentrate will return.

•*Are you having trouble with your outline or other reference material?*—Despite your preparation, something about the subject may interfere with your pace. If this is the case, it might pay to put the troublesome matter aside and turn to other material. Saving the difficult dictation for the end may give you a few minutes to reorganize without holding up your entire schedule.

3. Check Quality Factors

Some authors proceed at a pretty good clip and give every appearance of productive dictation. But even though their pace is satisfactory, in the end they lose the time-saving benefit because the quality of the dictated material makes heavy editing necessary. Some editing is unavoidable. However, if you can take stock of the quality factors, minimizing those that are undesirable and maximizing those that improve your performance, that's progress.

•*Are you sticking to the facts?*—This doesn't mean you have to leave them bare. Bare facts don't always communicate. You have to dress them up so that your meaning comes through in the way you want. For example, in order for a fact to be understood, you may have to explain why, such as with the statement, "Everyone must report to Personnel at nine o'clock Monday morning." When you add the reason— ". . . to get your permanent parking space assignments"—the information is now in perspective and understood.

•*Do you avoid wandering?*—In some cases, a dictater may stick with the outline and still be producing copy that will have to be heavily edited. It may happen because the point made by the cue or outline item is lost momentarily. The word originator digresses, adds thoughts that are only minimally relevant, or even off the track.

•*Do you avoid undesirable loading?*—This time-waste factor involves going into too much detail on a point, perhaps a minor one that need only be stated rather than elaborated. For example:

> Sales Manager Harry Greene dictates a memo and wants to emphasize to his field salespeople the need for visuals in their presentations to prospects. He says, ". . . and you all know the importance of using the charts and photos in the standard presentation. Repeated testing shows that those who use these have a higher sales-to-calls ratio than those who don't."

If Harry Greene stopped there and went on to his next point, he'd be O.K. But he continues on, reminding his salespeople about the cost and trouble of developing the material, and thus, boring his audience and wasting his dictation time.

The final point about interferences with the quality of dictation has to do with procedure.

●*Are you providing sufficient direction to the transcriber?—* All the rules for instructing the person who will type your material should be followed. Special punctuation, a technical word not in the transcriber's vocabulary, and other points about your copy that are not clear to the transcriber may mean errors or omissions that perhaps unnecessarily require the copy to go back to the typist.

4. Make No Unnecessary Stops

You should arrange to have your phone answered, and make sure no routine callers interrupt while you dictate.

Generally, it's a good idea not to take a break until you start slowing down or fatigue sets in.

One effective manager has a cup of coffee handy when he dictates. He says he finds that when doing a difficult job, it's preferable to sip his coffee rather than take an unnecessary break.

5. Set Subgoals

One way to keep rolling is to divide a heavy dictating session into two or more parts. While you might be somewhat intimidated by finding yourself with two hours of dictation ahead of you, if you think of it as two one-hour sessions or four half-hours, the sub-units seem less overwhelming. By taking brief breaks after each subgoal has been reached, you have an energy boost as you start into the next session.

6. Stick to Your Outline

Remember, your outline is a track on which you're running. Presumably you have laid it down with a certain amount of care. Generally, it's unwise to abandon your outline unless you're quite certain that it is a constructive change rather than a momentary whim that you may have to undo later.

In other words, unless you're sure that there's something wrong with your outline, or that you can improve on it, go down your list of items, elaborating on each one. Concentrate on expressing or expounding, point by point, each element of your outline.

7. Push On

One thing that expert dictaters do that often sets them apart from others: They don't stop to select the right word or to rethink a decision they made earlier. As you dictate, don't waste time over a matter of punctuation, or even how a particular passage sounds. You'll be able to take care of these matters later on. In order for your dictation to really be an effective and time-saving technique, it's much better to skip points you can't put into words. Don't worry too much about verbal clarity and so on. You can come back to all this in the next step. Your major objective—and try not to have anything interfere with it—is to complete your first draft. Then you have something tangible to work with in your editing step.

Part III.
Four Key Steps

10.
Editing Your Copy

A widely held misconception about dictation is that you say it once and that finishes the job. This *may* be true. For example, a simple letter in the hands of an experienced dictater may not require any change. But for more complex or longer communications, editing or rewriting is an essential part of the writing operation. (Professional writers use the terms *editing* and *rewriting* interchangeably. The terms will be so used here, although *rewriting* suggests a greater degree of change in copy than the term *editing*.)

Rewriting is the means by which you turn a rough draft into a finished product. Inexperienced writers assume that the skill of writing lies in having such a great command of language that you start with the first sentence, proceed to the end, and there you have it—finished copy. *The opposite is often true*. The very best writers—de Maupassant, Tolstoy, Hemingway, and Faulkner—would do a second, third, even a fourth draft before they were satisfied.

Changing Your Role

When you dictate, you're in the role of author. Working to improve your first draft, you become an editor—that is to say a critical reader. In this role, you pass judgment on what you have actually said. It's important to avoid being confused by any recollection of what you *intended* to say. Your own words in black and white are the materials you work with.

As you go through the copy, there are two general qualities that you evaluate: *sense* and *feeling*.

1. Sense

Is the thought that you wanted to express clear? And will it be clear to the person or the audience to whom the communication is addressed? For example, Manager Pearl Simmons has written an important memo to a subordinate. In the memo, she talks about starting from scratch to reconsider a situation, and she has dictated: "In a way, what I'm suggesting is similar to ZBB . . ."

To Simmons, ZBB means zero base budgeting, an approach with which she's familiar. But she realizes that as apt as her simile may be, it's going to confuse her subordinate rather than make a point, and so she deletes the ZBB reference and substitutes a sentence:

> "What I'm suggesting is that you forget about the present situation and its complications. Just start from scratch, noting your objectives and working backwards to the methods by which they can be achieved."

Another example, in which Helen Miller catches an implied thought of which she was unaware during dictation:

> "Henry, although we have worked together for several years, there still remains a large gap in our communications, though I have done my best to prevent it. Whenever possible, I have refrained from taking any actions that might affect you without first discussing the moves with you . . ."

On reading the copy, Helen Miller realizes that what she has written implies that while she has attempted to remedy the communications problem, Henry hasn't—which isn't true. Accordingly, she changes the phrase, "I have done my best," to "we have done our best," and the sense is both closer to the truth and makes for a more constructive statement.

To make sense, your facts must be correct. "Last week I . . ." dictates a department head. But the move he is referring to took place two weeks ago. The recipient might well be confused if he recalls the timing correctly. Is the writer talking about another incident that happened just last week?

In your editing, try to make your statements of fact as unambiguous and specific as possible: "The date was Tuesday, July 17th" . . . "The three people in attendance were Paul, Henrietta and Bill" . . . "The inspection turned up 167 rejects." Make changes, and check data that can sharpen your statements. Editing provides opportunity to review and tighten, to verify what has been said. Take advantage of this opportunity.

2. Feeling

Most communication has some kind of tone or feeling. In business, as in your personal world, feeling can run the gamut of emotion, from anger to enthusiasm, from argument to accord.

As you read your copy, judge the *feeling* content. For example:

• *Downbeat, negative*—"Although belated, this report seeks to face up to some problems . . . ." Is the phrase "although belated" necessary? Perhaps it is meant to reprove someone. Is that the feeling you want to convey? If not, the words should come out. And then, "seeks to face up to" sounds carping. Would the feeling of that opening be improved—from the viewpoint of the reader—if it simply read, "This report deals with problems . . ."?

• *Over-enthusiasm*—"I am sure that this approach can't help but be successful beyond our wildest expectations. . . ."

If you decided to bring that sentence down to earth by using moderate wording, it might read: "There seems little question that this approach, if correctly applied, could succeed perhaps better than anything attempted before . . . ."

•*Anger*—"Hell will freeze over before I agree to let you use the B building for storage. That's my facility . . ."
Anger is as valid an emotion as any other, and should not necessarily be throttled down. But since it is often temporary, it is unwise to give it the permanence of the written word. The idea expressed above can be stated in more temperate and acceptable terms: "I can't agree to let you use the B building for storage. That's my facility, and it is at full capacity right now."

In short, as you read, editing as you go, look not only for the obvious—typographical errors (typos), misspelling, and so on—but also for general effects of both the *sense* of what you've said and its *feeling* tone.

Key Points to Check

There are some general points to consider as you continue to edit your copy.

1. Is the Form Right?

We're not talking about details, but the overall structure of your piece. If it is a report, for example, have you organized the material in a way that will make it easy to read and easy to understand? Does each subsection have a descriptive heading? If appropriate, did you number the section, a device that always helps a reader stay oriented?

2. Is the Draft the Proper Length?

In some cases an outline may not give you a clue as to how long or short your draft will be. You may end up with a much longer or shorter report than anticipated. And length may be an important feature. For example, a serious subject, requiring considerable information and detail, might seem to be getting skimpy treatment if the draft runs to four or five pages. Perhaps twice that many are required to do justice to the subject.

In some cases, brevity rather than length may be desired. If your draft runs to 20 pages and the subject can be done full justice in 5, there's obviously a lot of padding or unnecessary material that you may want to edit out.

3. Have You Expressed Your Thoughts?

When you planned this report, you had certain intentions about what the report should say, points you wanted to cover, arguments you wanted to advance, suggestions you wanted to make. Does your draft do justice to your intentions?

4. Did You Pinpoint the Subject?

This often means putting it in perspective, explaining its importance, and so on. Notice, that "important" can mean different things. Important to him? To the company? To you? To others?

5. What About Repetition?

Don't assume that repetition must automatically be eliminated. Sometimes there is a good reason for repeating yourself. But if you do so, be sure you know why:

•*For emphasis*—To make an important point stand out, you may be perfectly justified in repeating. But, be sure it really is important.

•*For clarity*—You may want to repeat an old point in a new context to make sure your reader will understand. You can't risk the possibility that he has forgotten the point, or that he may fail to make the connection. So it may be wise to do your reader the courtesy of saying, "As I pointed out before . . . ." But, if you find too many "as I mentioned earlier's," it may signal the need for reorganization.

6. Can You Use One Word Instead of Two?

Extra words are excess baggage. In business especially, it's best to "travel light." When you read over your first draft, concentrate on eliminating heavy phrases. Here are some of the worst offenders:

Heavy	Light
accompanied by	with
afford an opportunity	allow
at all times	always
at this point in time	now
due to the fact that	because
experience has indicated that	we learned
in the near future	soon
in regard to	about
meets with our approval	we approve
prior to	before
subsequent to	after

7. Any Omissions?

Check to see if you have omitted any vital points. The test is whether you have left out anything that the reader needs to know.

Omissions usually occur because the writer is so steeped in his material that he assumes everybody else knows the details. Among the most common errors in this respect are:

1. Failure to identify people mentioned.
2. Failure to include definitions of unfamiliar terms that are used.
3. Failure to describe equipment or procedures involved in the situations under discussion.

8. Does the Idea Pass the Relevancy Test?

In rereading, one of your primary objectives should be to cut out as much material as you can. But how can you decide what to drop? Ask yourself: "Is this necessary in order to convey my basic idea? Does it add in understanding, or supply a key point?"

Remember that many things you might include in conversation have no place in a written report:

"I was talking about this with John—I ran into him in the washroom—and I found that we have the same problem of untrained help." Compare that with the speed and ease of understanding in: "John and I both have the same problem of untrained help."

9. How About the Flow of Ideas?

This point can best be understood if you examine the following memo. We have numbered the sentences for easy reference:

(1) We could arrange with Billing for part-time use of their calculating machine. (2) We have a girl who is capable of using the machine. (3) The workload on our present calculator is more than it can handle. (4) The Billing supervisor says it would be O.K. with her. (5) The overload is not enough to warrant a second machine as yet.

Obviously, one idea does not lead logically to the next. As an exercise in editing, rearrange the sentences by just listing in the margin the numbers in the order you prefer. (Here's a suggested sequence which may not make great literature but does make an intelligible paragraph: 3, 5, 1, 4, 2.)

In your own writing, you will rarely have to do more than rearrange a few sentences, if you outlined the material in advance.

This check on the sequence of sentences within each paragraph is important. It saves your reader the trouble of having to rearrange your ideas. In many cases, he may not do it; he'll just give up.

10. Do You Have a Good Conclusion?

People tend to remember the last thing they hear or read. Your conclusion makes the final impression. As you reread it, ask yourself what it accomplishes. Does it nail down your basic point? Keep in mind the main purpose behind your writing. Is it to inform, to ask information, or to produce action?

There are as many purposes as there are motives in human beings. Your conclusion, directly or indirectly, must reflect your purpose.

In judging your final draft—if it's a long or crucial communication—you don't have to go it alone. Remember, books often contain an acknowledgment. Many a writer's wife, children, friends, and colleagues have been asked to read drafts to pretest the writing for clarity, interest, and impact. If you like, get a second opinion about your writing as an assist in putting it into final shape. A friend and colleague, or a spouse who can be objective because of separation from the scene, may be just right for this assignment.

11. Any Second Thoughts?

Perhaps your outline reflected your best thinking at the time. But your project is at the stage now where rethinking makes it possible to come up with additional ideas that can further strengthen your copy. For example:

> Manager Al Gurney is reading a draft of a proposal for changing a work procedure in his department. He's done a good job of putting his ideas into words. But suddenly it strikes him that the addition of visual material—photos of the present setup, sketches showing the proposed improvements—would improve the impact of the proposal considerably.

Afterthoughts may be added at this stage of your writing if you take the time to make an overall review of your draft. Of course, this step is most appropriate for especially important pieces of dictation. Ordinary memos, letters, and so on can be adequately taken care of by going directly into the final editing step; crucial material may be edited two or more times.

Getting Down to the Finer Points

As you read your copy, keep an eye out for the three opportunities.

1. Deletions

You want to take out unnecessary words, phrases, sentences, and paragraphs. For example,

(before):

> "I'm very very enthusiastic. . . ."
> "You will find perhaps to your surprise that it is easy to match the two color samples."
> "I have had many second thoughts and must say that up to this very moment, I am not sure that the correct decision has been made in the Hadley matter."

(after):

> "I am enthusiastic."
> "It should be easy to match the two color samples."
> "I have had many second thoughts and I am still not sure that the Hadley matter has been decided correctly."

Proofreader's Marks

Marginal Mark	Instruction	Mark in Text	Corrected Text
ℐ	Delete	editor/	editor
ℐ̃	Delete and close up	bibßliography	bibliography
t/	Insert additional material in margin	typeseter ∧	typesetter
stet	Retain crossed out material	specifications and design of a book.	specifications and design of a book.
X	Broken type	booksⓔⓛⓛer	bookseller
‖	Align vertically	‖Gulf ‖ Publishing ‖ Company	Gulf Publishing Company
⁋	Start new paragraph	the original. Two photocopies are	the original. Two photocopies are
nw ⁋	Run on. No new paragraph	and printed. Then the signatures	and printed. Then the signatures
tr	Transpose words or letters indicated	Graphs should be on plotted	Graphs should be plotted on
⌒	Close up. No space	hand book	handbook
#	Insert space	bookclub	book club
⊐ ⊏	Center	⊐Preface⊏	Preface
⊐	Move to the right	and manuscript.⊐	and manuscript.
⊏	Move to the left	⊏A line drawing.	A line drawing
?	Is this correct?	not impossible	not possible
caps	Capitals	william shakespeare	William Shakespeare
lc	Lower case	Havre De Grace	Havre de Grace
rom	Roman	*first* printing	first printing
ital	Italic	in the Times	in the *Times*
bf	Bold face	Extra	**Extra**
⋀	Insert comma	composition printing ∧	composition, printing

Figure 10-1. Standard proofreading marks. (From the *Authors' Handbook*, 1976, Gulf Publishing Company, Houston, Texas)

2. Additions

You may want to add a qualifying word, or a sentence that makes a particular thought easier to grasp. For example, (before):

"We will have a regular company bus service from the station in White Plains to the plant, at 15-minute intervals. . ."

Marginal Mark	Instruction	Mark in Text	Corrected Text
;/	Insert semicolon	be displayed that is	be displayed; that is
:/	Insert colon	equation appears as follows	equation appears as follows:
⊙	Insert period	in your references	in your references.
?/	Insert question mark	When is permission required	When is permission required?
!/	Insert exclamation point	Stop the presses	Stop the presses!
/=/	Insert hyphen	paste up	paste-up
ᵛ	Insert apostrophe	Authors Handbook	Authors' Handbook
ᵛ ᵛ	Insert quotation marks	Make corrections in red, said the editor.	"Make corrections in red," said the editor.
ᵛ	Insert superior character	in his latest book	in his latest book^2
ᵥ	Insert inferior character	H$_2$O	H$_2$O
⊂/⊃	Insert parentheses	text see page 5	text (see page 5)
⊏/⊐	Insert brackets	n. d. 1850	n. d. [1850]
$\frac{1}{m}$	Insert one em dash	editor the person in	editor—the person in
sp	Spell out	abbr.	abbreviation
ld	Insert lead	appears as follows: abc = xyz	appears as follows: abc = xyz
out - see copy	There is an omission here. See copy	Occasionally, for use of copyrighted material.	Occasionally, copyright holders require payment for use of copyrighted material.
tr	Transfer to position shown by caret	prepare your manuscript carefully for mailing	carefully prepare your manuscript for mailing

Figure 10-1. (Continued.)

"May we please have everyone's cooperation on the litter problem? Halls and service rooms have been unsightly, due to the carelessness of a few employees."

(after)

"May we please have cooperation on the litter problem? Halls and service rooms have been unsightly."

3. Replacement

A word or phrase may be too strong, too weak, or insufficiently clear. You may strike out a word and use a synonym that comes closer to our meaning. For example,

(before):

"It's blood collection time again, and as in previous years, the Red Cross will set up a station in the cafeteria."

"I have today placed on Ray Lilly's broad and capable shoulders the responsibility for our Color Room operations."

(after):

"It's donor time again, and as in previous years, the Red Cross. . . " etc.

"I have today appointed Ray Lilly head of the Color Room operations."

Preparing Your Draft for Retyping

Professional writers use a set of symbols that simplifies correction of copy (Figure 10-1), shown on pages 116 and 117. Paragraphs that show how the marks are made on the first proof of a feature story are shown in Figure 10-2.

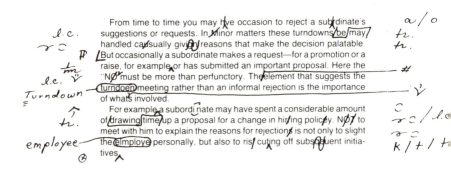

Figure 10-2. This sample proof shows how proofreading marks are used.

Don't worry about the number of symbols you see. In practice, you will probably find that some are rarely used. And your familiarity with 10 or 12 of the most commonly used marks will make correcting the draft easier. The people doing the typing in your WP center probably are familiar with the symbols. However, any common-sense way of correcting a draft will also be understood (until you gain familiarity with the standard symbols).

Part IV.
Increased Excellence

11.
Sharpening Your Skills

Whether you've had a great deal of experience in dictation or just a little, you may be interested in sharpening your skill. While experience is a good teacher, in the case of dictation, there are two dangers:

•*You've plateaued*—Analysis of the techniques of dicters suggests that there is a tendency to reach a particular level of performance and stay there. On this plateau, since it often represents a comfortable level, habit tends to keep the individual functioning in this familiar way. However, it's often possible to get off this learning plateau and move on to an even more satisfactory one.

•*Inefficient elements creep in*—A secretary told me, "My boss wastes about one-half hour out of every hour of dictation by injecting social conversation between letters and memos. It's not that I object to conviviality. It's just that it comes at an awkward time . . ."

There's a whole string of time-wasting practices that lie in wait for the unwary. The following pages can help you see how you're doing, and eliminate obstacles to improvement.

Assess Yourself

Three key points can help you evaluate how well you are dictating.

●*Output (quantity)*—Are you satisfied with the rate with which you are turning out copy? Do you feel your dictation is really doing what you expect of it—making a sizable reduction in the amount of time you spend writing?

●*Copy hardness (quality)*—This term refers to the degree to which writing is lean and to the point. Copy is hard if it avoids digression and verbosity, and does not require excessive editing. Below are two examples of copy. One is "soft," that is, longwinded and digressive. The second conveys the same message, streamlined.

Here is a message sent by one manager to another:

> Please afford my secretary an opportunity to check the Jones file. Since you at all times have cooperated with such requests, I hope you will acquiesce once more. Due to the fact that this information must be forthcoming in the near future, I trust you will be able to grant permission at your earliest convenience.

Here is the same memo as it should have been dictated:

> Do you mind letting my secretary check the Jones file? We need some information urgently and your help would be greatly appreciated.

If you think the first version above is exaggerated, of course you are right. But the sad fact is that it is representative of a large percentage of business writing.

To say of a dictater that he or she writes "hard copy" is high praise. While no one should expect to dictate perfect or *finished copy*, the less revision required, the more time saved.

•*Communication effectiveness*—The final point of judgment has to do with the appropriateness and impact of your dictation. Are you saying what you mean? Is the feeling tone right for the message? For example, is the letter to a customer simple and straightforward? Is the memo to a colleague friendly and informal?

Do you find a minimum of misunderstanding, or requests for clarification from people to whom you write?

Do you feel that you have a reputation for being a "good writer" in your organization?

Check Your Performance

The list of hangups may help you identify drags on your performance. The interesting thing about hangups is that they may become habitual, and people aren't even aware of them. A secretary told me:

> "My boss is a brilliant man and very imaginative. His brain always seems to be churning away, and his fantasizing often goes on during dictation. The result is, he stands up and goes wandering off to get a drink of water, to check something in the file unrelated to the dictation he is doing, and so on.
>
> "I mentioned this to him the other day and he was quite startled. As a matter of fact, he didn't believe that my description of his frequent breaks in dictation was accurate. He asked me, then, to call his attention to these interruptions.
>
> "The next dictating session, he had been going for only five minutes when he jumped up to rearrange a plant on the windowsill that caught his attention. I pointed out the interruption. He continued dictating. A few minutes later he was going through the books on his bookshelf, looking for an atlas to check on a trip he planned to make the following week. I saw the book he had taken out of the case and realized it had nothing to do with the dictation. When I pointed out the second interruption, he nodded rather coolly. By the time we ended, he had racked up five unnecessary stops.
>
> "'I guess you're right,'" he said. 'I didn't realize I was being so fidgety . . .'"

The point is not to criticize the erring executive, but to show that it is possible to indulge in counterproductive behavior during dictation and not realize it.

Below is a list of hangups that cut down on dictation efficiency, along with some suggested remedies. You may suffer from none of these, but going through the list may suggest others that once identified, might be eliminated.

•*Rambling and digression*—The solution here lies in closely following an outline. If you find you are straying, go over the outline to make sure it covers your subject adequately. Once verified, stick to it, forcing yourself to stop when you seem to be off the track.

•*It's disconcerting to come to a halt and have to grope for words*—Generally this hangup is the result of inexperience. As you practice and pick up speed, the frequency of "dead spots" will decrease. However, if the rapport between you and a secretary is poor, you may want to try other expedients. Switch to machine dictation, and see if that helps. Or if you can, dictate to someone else. Another possibility: let your secretary know that you don't expect to talk smoothly on a particular piece. If you are new to dictation, it is no disgrace to admit it. Your secretary should then find it easier to wait for you to gather your thoughts.

•*I never liked gadgets, and talking to a lifeless machine is disconcerting*—One solution would be to work with a secretary, if possible. Another solution may be new equipment if you dislike your particular model. Today's market offers a wide variety of machines. If you are having trouble with the one you've been using, look at a different model. It may minimize your problem.

•*I lose time trying to clarify what I want to say*—If this is your problem, bulling it through may be your solution. Dictate any word or phrase that *approximates* the sense or the idea you are trying to verbalize. Once you get over the hurdle, you can continue on, knowing that you will be able to improve the copy in the editing stage.

The important thing is to work towards a first draft. Once you have it, you have something to work with. If you stop often to mull over the wording of a statement or to find a sentence that precisely represents your idea, you're likely to be wasting time. However rough your draft, you at least have something to work with in the editing step. Then you can work on the phrase you are dissatisfied with, and can seek other choices until you find one that is satisfactory.

The point is worth repeating: Most good dictaters push on to complete their first drafts regardless of how many gaps or unsatisfactory words and sentences there may be in the copy. With the first draft done, you are in a much stronger position to make improvements.

Practice Sessions

Practice may or may not make perfect, but it does make for improvement. Your normal day-to-day experience in dictating can be an effective skill-builder. However, practice of elements in which you are less capable than you would like can improve overall results. Below are suggestions that can help you increase your skill.

Verbalizing

In dictating from notes or an outline, you clothe your ideas with words. Two ways in which to build this ability are:

•*Select your own previously-used material*—Go back to notes or outlines you have used in the past. Dictate from them using a recording machine if possible, so that you can practice dictationese and have a transcription made. Aim to make the flow of words smooth and coherent.

After the exercise, compare your practice session with the original effort. Do you feel the quality of the second attempt is better than the original?

If you can't get a copy of your original dictation, do the same material a second time from your notes, trying to dictate tighter copy with a better choice of words and a communication that in total is more effective. Do you feel you were able to improve? One of the benefits of this exercise is that you may see that there is more than one way to fill out an outline. This flexibility is an asset because it helps you break away from cliches and come up with fresh ways of expressing an idea. When your dictation becomes freer, even flamboyant, you are making real progress.

●*Devise outlines from current correspondence or projects—* A manager who had been developing a procedure to increase the efficiency of one of the operations in his department made up an outline for an interim report to submit to his boss.

> "I was doing it mainly to practice getting from the outline stage to a first draft. When I had the dictation transcribed, it sounded so good I labeled it 'An Interim Report' and sent it along to my boss."

You may not have a ready-made situation like the manager's, but in the same way, you can put down some cues or outlines for a communication, dictate from it, and either get it transcribed or listen to a recording to judge the quality of the piece. Is it coherent, clear, and interesting? Does it stick to the points you want to make? Which are the strong points of your dictation—arresting, persuasive, or dramatic? Are there any weak points—irrelevancies, murky sentences, dull portions?

If you are dissatisfied with a piece you've dictated, try it again, possibly revamping the outline to strengthen it. Compare the second attempt to the first. If you listened to or read the first version critically, the second try should be better.

Practice Outlining

You can test out and improve your ability to develop outlines in two ways:

•*Working from a finished piece*—Find an article or a report on a subject related to your work. Then, develop an outline from the material. For example, note the statement, or theme, or subject in the introduction. Then state the points made by the first copy after the introduction. In the same way, continue to fill out the outline on which the structure of the piece is based.

•*Make up outlines for general subjects*—There's an endless array of subjects that everyone is an "expert" on. Here are some suggestions:

1. Why I love my home town.
2. The best day I ever had in my working experience.
3. What makes a good subordinate?
4. My ideal kind of boss.

Devise an outline which will make it possible for you to express all your thoughts on the subject. (If you are having any trouble, check Chapter 7.)

Practice Dictationese

To add to your fluency in speaking dictationese, go through your files checking memos, letters, reports and other materials that lend themselves to dictation.

Then, as illustrated in Chapter 2, take the finished product and re-dictate it. Be sure to specify the format, correct spacing, punctuation—everything necessary to get you an exact copy of the document you're working from.

If you are using a long report, there is no need to go through the entire piece. Just dictate enough to get a fair sample of the original in terms of style.

For this exercise it would be especially helpful to have your dictationese transcribed. In this way, you will be able to make a point-by-point comparison with the original material. The points at which your version differs from the original probably are those where your dictationese was imperfect. Whatever the cause of the difference—for example, failure to spell out unusual words or names, or imperfect punctuation—these become things that you should take special care with in subsequent dictation.

Practice Editing

For this exercise, you can find raw material to work with almost anywhere. You may take a newspaper, magazine articles, or the richest source of all, your own files. The fact is, no piece of copy is likely to be perfect. Pencil in hand, read through sentences and paragraphs making the changes that you feel improve the copy.

If you use magazine articles, be sure to take nonfiction pieces. In fiction it might be argued that your changes destroy some subtle, literary quality. You stay away from this difficulty by avoiding any form of fiction.

On-the-Job Practice

If you use dictation in your present job, every time you push the *on* button of a recorder, or say, "Miss Smith, please take a letter," you are staging the best kind of practice session—getting experience in all the four steps mentioned previously.

How Do You Rate as a Dictater?

In appraising your skill, it is helpful to measure, however roughly, where you stand at present.

You may be new to the game or you may have been dictating for years. In either case, you probably have acquired a few habits that interfere with your effectiveness.

Here is a chance to review your dictating practices, and come up with a score that shows how you are doing. Of course, the point isn't to praise or find fault, but to help you spot specific points that can be improved.

The following questions hit some of the high spots. Answer the questions with one of four responses and add up your score:

Always = 5 points   Sometimes = 2 points
Mostly = 3 points   Never = 0 points

	Always	Mostly	Sometimes	Never
1. Are your dictation periods:				
a. Timed to allow leeway for transcription before the last mail?	( )	( )	( )	( )
b. At a time when other matters are under control so that you can concentrate on your dictation?	( )	( )	( )	( )
c. At a time when your personal energy is up to a level appropriate to the task at hand?	( )	( )	( )	( )
2. Do you make every effort to prevent unnecessary interruptions while dictating?	( )	( )	( )	( )

	Always	Mostly	Sometimes	Never
3. Do you have at your fingertips all the information you require for the dictation you plan to give?	( )	( )	( )	( )
4. Do you have your sequence of items for dictation set in advance, to minimize the paper shuffling you do once you get started?	( )	( )	( )	( )
5. Do you clearly state your instructions for each piece of dictated material— whether it's a memo, a letter, a report, or other type of communication?	( )	( )	( )	( )
6. Do you spell out unusually difficult words, proper names, and technical phrases, and repeat all critical figures?	( )	( )	( )	( )
7. Do you clearly state your priorities— which items are to be rushed, which can be left for last?	( )	( )	( )	( )
8. Do you ask for a rough draft when you anticipate changes in your copy?	( )	( )	( )	( )
9. Do you come through loud and clear when you dictate (as proved by the absence of queries about meaning, spelling or punctuation)?	( )	( )	( )	( )
10. Whether you work with a secretary or WP system, do you make, or go along with, simple rules of procedure so that a minimum of time need be devoted to routine matters?	( )	( )	( )	( )
11. Do you indicate corrections clearly, preferably using proofreaders' marks, so that a third draft isn't needed?	( )	( )	( )	( )
12. Generally, do you find it unnecessary for:				
a. Routine memos and letters to be sent back for correction?	( )	( )	( )	( )

	Always	Mostly	Sometimes	Never
b. Difficult material to require more than a single editing before final copy?	( )	( )	( )	( )
13. Would you say you have a good working relationship with your secretary or those who do your transcribing?	( )	( )	( )	( )
14. When you speak dictationese, do you signal the secretary or transcriber by voice modulation, or direct address when giving instructions?	( )	( )	( )	( )
15. Do you try to keep your outlines as simple as possible, in order to give full play to your spontaneous verbalizing?	( )	( )	( )	( )

Interpretation

Please remember that there is nothing scientific about this quiz. At best, it aims to furnish you with a rough measure of your dictation performance by rating you on some of the key points on which good dictation practice rests.

• *80 to 90*—You have every reason to be pleased with your dictating ability. The only suggestion for those who fall into this group, and it is the one that experts in work effectiveness always make, is that you make sure the time you save in dictation is applied to other key parts of your job. This way you are sure to get the payoff you've earned by your dictation skill.

• *70 to 79*—This range indicates good proficiency, that perhaps with just a little more effort can put the dictater into the top group.

An obvious way to improve your skill is to go back over your answers, noting where you scored less than five points.

These areas have room for improvement.

For example: Question 2 addresses itself to your handling of interruptions. A low score suggests that you are being impeded by stops and starts that cut down on your effectiveness. Any effort you make to bar the people or events that needlessly break into your dictation sessions will pay off in elimination of time waste.

Each low score affords a similar potential for improvement in the area on which the question focusses.

•*60 to 69*—This is merely a get-by level. The bright side, for those who rate in this range, is that there are many ways to improve. Go back over the quiz, and check off the questions answered *Sometimes* or *Never*. Each of these can steer you towards a specific practice that will benefit from remedial attention. Tackle two or three at a time, trying to make the improvement during your actual dictating sessions.

•*Below 60*—If you scored below 60, and are new to the game, then the likelihood is that you will benefit greatly from practice. But make sure that you don't include in your dictation routine, inefficient habits that slow you down, or otherwise depress the quality of your dictation.

People in this group who have been dictating for some time might benefit from a total refresher. Go back to the beginning, review all your dictating procedures—possibly with the help of this book—and try to eliminate the bad while incorporating the good into your new approach.

Another suggestion: The quiz questions touch on only some of the highspots of dictation practice. Try to use each dictation period on the job as a learning experience. Concentrate on what you are doing, and if it's in the cards, discuss either with your secretary or people in the WP unit, the things you can do to make their job easier.

In some cases, a reason for poor performance may be the relatively small amount of time you spend on dictation during a typical work week. But don't be content to fumble and grope on the assumption that "It really doesn't matter because I dictate so seldom." You might be losing a skill that could be a career boost in the years ahead.

Part IV.
Increased Excellence

12.
Additional Uses of Dictation

In mastering dictation for day-to-day working purposes, the word originator is in the happy position of having a skill that, like those famous Swiss army knives, turns out to have many uses. Accordingly, as you master the art of dictation, particularly if you become familiar with machine recording, you may find it has applications that can bring additional benefits, even remuneration.

This concluding chapter suggests how your "writing-out-loud" ability can be used as a means of:

1. Idea clarification
2. Recording personal history
3. Professional writing
4. Speech writing and rehearsal

Idea Clarification

It's a story you may have heard before, but it has special application here:

"What do you think about the issue at hand, Mr. Smith?"
"I don't know. I haven't said anything about it yet."

The point of the anecdote is that the act of speaking itself is a factor in forming an idea, taking a glimmering of a thought and giving it substance.

One executive recounts this incident:

"I was scheduled to attend a meeting on a crucial matter of company policy. For weeks there had been exchanges on an informal basis as to whether we should or shouldn't open a new plant on the East Coast. There were proponents and opponents, and strong arguments both for and against the move. And here I was, set to enter a meeting the next day, and I still wasn't sure in my own mind where I stood. I decided to make up two arguments, one for the move and one against. I made up two brief outlines and then proceeded to make my presentations—to my desk tape recorder.

"As I spoke, going along the track suggested by each outline, thoughts that I had not fully resolved got straightened out as I gave them expression. And related ideas that I hadn't thought of came to mind. I included them into my recording. At the end of the dictation session, I had pretty well thought through all my ideas and feelings, pro and con. When I played back the tapes, I discovered that almost all my ideas had crystallized. I felt that there were one or two points that I had not addressed myself to satisfactorily. On the playback, I had the chance to reconsider and develop them.

"As a result of this exercise, I entered the meeting in a much better position to understand both points of view. Just in passing, I should add that as a result of the verbalizing, I had come to feel that the move did seem to have more advantages than disadvantages, and that was the view I backed in the discussion."

For those who have made dictation a dependable skill and who like the experience of applying this skill to clarifying points of view or judgments, dictation makes it possible to move ahead to the point where inconclusive thinking is replaced by a clear-cut decision or opinion.

Several participants in the workshop group were interested enough in the possibilities of idea clarification to try it for themselves. Some subjects and problems they discussed were:

1. Early retirement. This is a subject where the increase in objectivity you achieve by listening to your views as played back on a tape can be a real help in unkinking some of the knots that may exist.
2. Why am I so upset? One participant, usually of a sunny disposition, had quarreled with one of his colleagues who, he felt, had palmed off an unpleasant assignment on him. The colleague protested that their supervisor had given the job to the participant instead of to him because he was busy with another priority task. The participant had rejected that explanation: "You just played being busy. You'd have taken that job if it weren't one of the dogs . . ." The participant recounted the situation to a recording machine, trying his best to describe the disagreement fairly. Listening to the playback, he decided that possibly, he had jumped the gun. His colleague's explanation could have been true. As a result, he decided to try to restore the relationship, since his upset was largely due to his unhappiness at the possibility of losing a friend.
3. Promotions. A supervisor needed an assistant, and his boss gave him the go-ahead. There were two logical candidates among departmental employees. Both were capable but their abilities were quite different. Pete was bright, knew the work, but tended to forget details. Helen was very good at details, had better educational qualifications than Pete, and while not quite as experienced as the other candidate, was quick to learn. The supervisor listed the pros and cons of each candidate in a "thinking out loud" session. After the playback (he made notes while listening), he decided that in the long run, Helen would be the better choice.

The advantage of the dictating session was that it forced him to think about the two candidates in an objective way, and to be specific about pro and con feelings.

Recording Personal History

With the interest in our ancestry sparked by Alex Hailey's *Roots*, recording offers a new way to put into permanent form your personal or family history.

Strictly speaking, it is not so much your ability to dictate as to use a recorder that opens up the possibilities of a personal or family history. With the machine at the ready, you may undertake informal interviews with family members, particularly the older ones who are a repository of memories which only they witnessed or can recall.

Professional Writing

A sufficient number of books have been produced with the "as told to" tag. The general public is led to believe that a large number of writers are supported by the rich and famous who employ writers (and their tape recorders) to assist in getting their reminiscences published.

Perhaps you are not interested in the "as told to" collaboration. But people with something to say, a story to tell, or ideas to express, may be able to "write" their pieces into a recorder when they are deterred by the process of writing by typewriter or longhand.

The virtue of dictating a piece of fiction or nonfiction lies in being able to produce a first draft. Once you have some version of your piece down on paper, it becomes possible for you, working with that material, to do the editing, revision, and polishing that gives a final, and possibly publishable, piece of writing.

Please understand that this is not to be construed as a general invitation to all comers to take the plunge into print. The job of professional writing requires much more than an ability to string words together. But, if you have the interest, and at least a core of talent, you may find it a fascinating adventure to test out that barely-repressed urge to have a short story, novel, or play with your name on it printed and published. The ability to dictate simply makes the mechanical part of writing—getting words on paper—considerably easier.

Speech Writing and Rehearsal

From time to time, you may be called on to make a speech, or, as it is sometimes put, "to say a few words" at a public gathering. Let me tell you how a friend of mine, a management consultant, uses his experience with dictation to carry out such an assignment.

"First of all," he says, "I research the subject, look through my own notes and files, and get books or magazine articles. Then I check back to the kind of audience I'll be addressing.

"When I feel I have a good handle on what I want to say, I make an outline, as brief as possible. Then I find a quiet room, turn on my recorder, and using my outline, I 'talk' my speech. I try to stick with my outline, but I often find that I add other points and ideas as I dictate.

"I have the recording transcribed, and then edit that—adding, deleting, refining. Now, if I'm lucky, after retyping I have a finished draft.

"Again, I go off with my recorder, and now read my speech, doing it pretty much as I expect to when I'm really on. Then I play it back. I time it, and make notes to sharpen up a point here or there. My speech is ready. I don't read it to the audience—that's deadly. But what I do is to re-outline the final draft, and stay, in a general way, with it. I may take the final version with me to the dais, and keep it handy for one or two crucial points that I read verbatim, to make *sure* I get them *exactly* right."

My friend's procedure is one possible way to use your dictating experience as an assist to speech writing or delivery. I do some public speaking from time to time, and proceed somewhat differently. After getting a satisfactory outline, I give the speech and record it. I don't have a transcription made, but play it back, and make notes on my outline. Then I feel I'm prepared. In some cases, I give the speech a second time, including the material suggested by my notes. On the playback, I listen for such things as emphasis and change of pace. If I feel there are dull passages—there often are—I will either trim them down or try to add material that will liven up the section.

In one or two cases, I have suggested to people who have trouble speaking in public to make up a brief talk on any subject on which they feel well informed. Then, record the talk, and have a few friends or family members listen, along with the speaker, to the playback. If the audience has been well selected, a discussion about the talk can give the would-be speechmaker useful feedback on both strong and weak points. If the first session is successful, one or two additional sessions, preferably on other subjects, should give the individual the experience that will make the real thing easier to take.

Improving Quantity

The applications just described, as well as any other uses you can dream up for your dictation have a hidden value. Regardless of the direct purposes of these nonbusiness uses, an indirect benefit is to help you improve your skill by extending your experience. The more the dictation process becomes second nature—particularly when the material requires that you speak dictationese and intersperse text with instructions to the transcriber—the greater your mastery will be.

Above and beyond the objective targets of improvement, quantity and quality, there is a third goal. Although subjective, it is not to be overlooked. Quite simply, it is the enjoyment of the dictation experience. After all, when you dictate, you are expressing yourself. And self-expression can be an ego-involving and ego-soothing activity.

Important Features

Index